STUDIES IN ENGLISH LITERATURE No. 11

General Editor

David Daiches

Professor of English
and
Dean of the School of English and American Studies
University of Sussex

GEORGE ELIOT:
MIDDLEMARCH

by
DAVID DAICHES

EDWARD ARNOLD (PUBLISHERS) LTD.
41 Maddox Street, London W.1

First published 1963
Reprinted 1965

Printed in Great Britain by
Butler & Tanner Ltd., Frome and London

General Preface

It has become increasingly clear in recent years that what both the advanced Sixth Former and the university student need most by way of help in their literary studies are close critical analyses and evaluations of individual works. Generalisations about periods or authors, general chat about the Augustan Age or the Romantic Movement, have their uses; but often they provide merely the illusion of knowledge and understanding of literature. All too often students come up to the university under the impression that what is required of them in their English literature courses is the referring of particular works to the appropriate generalisations about the writer or his period. Without taking up the anti-historical position of some of the American 'New Critics', we can nevertheless recognise the need for critical studies that concentrate on the work of literary art rather than on its historical background or cultural environment.

The present series is therefore designed to provide studies of individual plays, novels and groups of poems and essays, which are known to be widely studied in Sixth Forms and in universities. The emphasis is on clarification and evaluation; biographical and historical facts, while they may of course be referred to as helpful to an understanding of particular elements in a writer's work, will be subordinated to critical discussion. What kind of work is this? What exactly goes on here? How good is this work and why? These are the questions which each writer will try to answer.

DAVID DAICHES

Middlemarch

I

The full title of the book is 'Middlemarch, a Study of Provincial
Life', and this provides certain directions for reading. We must not
expect concentration on the fortunes of a single hero. This novel is
to be concerned with a community, with inter-relationships, with
individual response to social pressures and the effect of society on
individual ambitions. Yet as soon as we turn over the title-page and
encounter the Prelude, it seems as though these expectations are to be
frustrated. The novel, the Prelude suggests, is to be about the idealistic hopes and socially compelled frustrations of a latter-day Saint
Theresa. The tone of these three introductory paragraphs is oddly
compounded of compassionate admiration and irony. The author
looks back on the little Theresa and her brother going out to seek
martyrdom: 'Out they toddled from rugged Avila, wide-eyed and
helpless-looking as two fawns, but with human hearts,[1] already beat-
ing to a national idea; until domestic reality met them in the shape of
uncles, and turned them back from their great resolve.' Words like
'toddled' and 'domestic reality' sound faintly mocking. The mockery
seems to disappear in the second paragraph, where George Eliot talks
of 'these later-born Theresas' who are 'helped by no coherent social
faith and order which could perform the function of knowledge for
the ardently willing soul'. And in the last paragraph she declares herself even more distinctly, at the same time introducing water imagery
('pond', 'stream') which is to be used several times throughout the
novel to suggest the varying possibilities open to the individual of
directing and expanding the meaning of his life:

Here and there a cygnet is reared uneasily among the ducklings in

[1] The editions of 1871, 1872 and 1873 read 'distinctively human
hearts'. George Eliot removed the adverb in making revisions for the
1874 edition, which is the one used here.

the brown pond, and never finds the living stream in fellowship with its own oary-footed kind. Here and there is born a Saint Theresa, foundress of nothing, whose loving heart-beats and sobs after an unattained goodness tremble off and are dispersed among hindrances, instead of centring in some long-recognisable deed.

The author seems emotionally committed here, yet the ugly duckling analogy and such a phrase as 'its own oary-footed kind' still keep up a suspicion of irony, while the phrase 'foundress of nothing' could be read equally as compassionate or deflating.

These ambiguities of tone represent something fundamental to the novel, in which irony and compassion are used together more consistently than critics have noted—one might, for example, profitably go through the book and note the different inflections with which the word 'poor' is used in its frequent association with the main characters, 'poor Dorothea', 'poor Mr. Casaubon', 'poor Rosamund', 'poor Lydgate'—but the question remains why George Eliot should have prefaced her novel with a statement which suggests that its main theme is the frustration of a modern Theresa, who is of course Dorothea Brooke, when both the title of the novel and its scope and structure suggest otherwise. Is the Prelude to be read simply as an introduction to Book I, which is indeed centred on Dorothea? Or does it represent a temporary surrender on the author's part to that aspect of the novel which had most relevance to her own early life and ambitions? The latter suggestion is probably the truer. Most critics rightly feel uncomfortable about it. In its ambiguity of tone it is relevant and helpful, but in its suggestion of theme it is far too limiting. *Middlemarch* is a more complex, more subtle and more interesting novel than the Prelude might suggest.

Book I is the only section of *Middlemarch* where the title—simply 'Miss Brooke'—does not suggest the interweaving of the different strands of which the novel is composed. The four main areas of interest—Dorothea and Casaubon, Lydgate and Rosamund, Bulstrode, and Fred Vincy and the Garths—are inter-related with great skill as the story proceeds, but at the beginning we focus on Dorothea. Actually, the Lydgate-Rosamund story was the one which George Eliot first thought of, and she began writing in 1869 with the account of Lydgate which was probably the same as that which now forms chapter 15. The following year she had an idea for another story, to be called at first 'Miss Brooke', which was conceived quite independently. The two stories were fused early in 1871, and we can see the fusion very deftly carried out in the dinner-party gossip of chapter 10. But the origins and development of the novel are of only minor critical interest. The novel as we have it is the product of its author's mature vision of the mutual interaction between different lives in a given society. If Book I focuses on Dorothea that is because the reader must be firmly drawn into the story through involvement with the fate of a richly presented individual before he is in a position to enlarge his gaze and see the wider pattern of human action and reaction. This funnel technique, as it may be called, is especially important where the novelist does not present the action consistently through the point of view of one of his characters, but employs the 'omniscient author' method. The omniscient author, just because he is free to look anywhere and say anything, has the greater responsibility to funnel his material in at first through a single narrow entry. If we remain with the sensibility and consciousness of an individual character, we can extend our gaze very widely at once, for the controlling consciousness of the observer will concentrate and order the picture for us. But when the author's awareness remains above and around his characters, always available to the reader, and expansion of meaning can always be achieved by author's comment, he cannot risk dissipating the effect of the opening chapters by trying to cover too much human material.

The opening description of Dorothea Brooke is a brilliant set piece. Her birth, her environment, her way of life, her relations with her sister Celia, are all presented in a sequence of sharply defined sentences, and the imagery from the outset ('Blessed Virgin', 'Italian painters', 'quotation from the Bible', 'paragraph of today's newspapers') suggest that disparity between character and environment which is to play such an important part in Dorothea's story and at the same time sets going suggestions that are to be fruitfully utilised later. The true direction of this opening paragraph is not, however, fully revealed until we come to the sentence: 'Dorothea knew many passages of Pascal's *Pensées* and of Jeremy Taylor by heart; and to her the destinies of mankind, seen by the light of Christianity, made the solicitudes of feminine fashion appear an occupation for Bedlam.' The violence of that final word 'Bedlam' brings us up short. We are made to sense a disproportion, a touch even, almost, of hysteria, about Dorothea's absorption in such improbable (for a young girl) authors as Pascal and Jeremy Taylor. In the light of this, what follows is curiously ambivalent, and on the whole more critical than admiring:

> Her mind was theoretic, and yearned by its nature after some lofty conception of the world which might frankly include the parish of Tipton and her own rule of conduct there; she was enamoured of intensity and greatness, and rash in embracing whatever seemed to her to have those aspects; likely to seek martyr-dom, to make retractions, and then to incur martyrdom after all in a quarter where she had not sought it.

'Theoretic' and 'rash' are the adjectives that strike us here. The former suggests—and the suggestion is soon developed in a great variety of ways—that Dorothea did not really know the world she lived in; that her actions and attitudes were based on general ideas that had never been tested by experience and indeed had never been fully examined intellectually. From one point of view, and in one of its aspects, *Middlemarch* is a *Bildungsroman*, a novel, that is, in which the heroine (in so far as she is the heroine) is educated by life into a fuller knowledge of herself and her relation to her environment. Self-knowledge, and the development of a sense of true vocation, are for George Eliot the proper objects of all human questing, and characters are judged by the degree to which they achieve them. One might perhaps say that the grand theme of *Middlemarch* concerns problems of self-knowledge and vocation in a context of society at work. Dorothea, it is suggested, lacks self-knowledge and has al-together unreal ideas about her true or her possible relation to her environment.

The second paragraph of this chapter introduces us to Mr. Brooke, Dorothea's uncle, a man 'of acquiescent temper, miscellaneous opinions, and uncertain vote'. This summary description will be given much fuller meaning in later episodes, where Mr. Brooke's conversation and actions (but especially the former) will illustrate precisely what George Eliot means by these three phrases. The immediate account is enough to go on. The author draws attention to Mr. Brooke's combination of benevolent intentions and miserly habits before ending this paragraph with a generalisation to which she moves easily from the description: 'For the most glutinously indefinite minds enclose some hard grains of habit; and a man has been seen lax about all his own interests except the retention of his snuff-box, concerning which he was watchful, suspicious, and greedy of clutch.' We shall have to examine later the function of such generalisations in the novel. There are many of them, and they always emerge by way of comment on or illustration of a particular action or situation that has just been presented. Some of them have the ring of proverbs, while others seem more like intensely personal discoveries. They rarely point the moral of what has just occurred in the novel; rather, they refer the action to some generalisation which may help to explain it or, more often, relate it to some widespread characteristics of human beings as moral creatures. Their function is to broaden the application of the particular event, not crudely to tell the reader what to think about it.

Even in this brief paragraph about him, we are given notice that Mr. Brooke is to be in considerable measure a comic character. And when, later on, we become familiar with his characteristic method of expressing himself, culminating in the magnificent comic scene of his electioneering speech in chapter 51, we may be led to think of him as a kind of Dickensian humorous eccentric. But the deliberate ambiguity of George Eliot's attitude to her principal characters extends to Mr. Brooke. He is foolish, even ridiculous, and often very funny; yet, as we shall see, what he says often hits on an essential truth—even, on occasion, an essential wisdom—that none of the wiser characters in the novel can reach. In an introductory chapter an author cannot deploy all her resources of irony and complexity, she can only give notice of them. The focus here is on Dorothea, and here the complexities are indeed suggested; on other points George Eliot contents herself with bare outlines which are to be filled in, sometimes in very unexpected ways, later on.

Another important theme is introduced in this opening chapter: this is the relation of the characters to their historical past and to the moment of history in which they are now living. Mr. Brooke, we are told, gave no evidence of the hereditary strain of Puritan energy, 'but in his niece Dorothea it glowed alike through faults and virtues'.

Earlier, we had been told of a Puritan Brooke ancestor who served under Cromwell. The Brookes are part of English history as well as part of English society (and the pattern of society is also bound up with history). The past and the present, the individual and society, are deftly brought together in this third paragraph of chapter 1, which concludes with a reference to Mr. Brooke's estate, 'presumably worth about three thousand a-year—a rental which seemed wealth to provincial families still discussing Mr. Peel's late conduct on the Catholic Question, innocent of future gold-fields, and of that gorgeous plutocracy which has so nobly exalted the necessities of genteel life'. This shows at once that the author is looking back from the vantage point of her own time to the period of the novel, which is in fact quite precisely dated by references to historical events as extending from 30 September 1829 to the end of May 1832.[1] *Middlemarch* is not only about Dorothea and Casaubon and Lydgate and other characters; it is also about provincial English society on the eve of the Reform Bill of 1832. The movement of history surrounds the characters, and impinges on their destinies often in odd or oblique or unrealised ways. Will Ladislaw's political journalism for Mr. Brooke, for example, is made possible by the electioneering that followed the dissolution of Parliament on 22 April 1831 as a result of the *impasse* with respect to the Reform Bill. Each individual horizon —even Dorothea's—is bounded by its own interests, and sees history in the making only in the degree to which the individual's hopes or fears are affected. This is how history affects contemporaries. By looking back from 1870 on to 1829-32, the author can see as a historical movement what to her characters were merely fragmentary events that helped or hindered their own ambitions, and this makes a special kind of irony possible. The omniscient author is omniscient in three dimensions—psychologically, in knowing what goes on inside her characters' consciousnesses; in space, in knowing what is going on in different places at the same time; and in time, in

[1] See 'History by Indirection: the Era of Reform in *Middlemarch*', by Jerome Beaty. *Victorian Studies*, I, 2, pp. 173-9. This article brings together all the historical references in the novel, and dates them precisely. The author shows how, by using historical material indirectly but with absolute precision, George Eliot gives extra scope and depth to her fiction.

knowing how the historical pattern in which the characters are unwittingly involved is really shaped. Yet George Eliot does not abuse
her position. She is not *complacently* ahead of her characters in time,
as her reference to 'that gorgeous plutocracy which has so nobly
exalted the necessities of genteel life' makes quite clear. She is ambivalent about progress, as about other matters.

We return in the fourth paragraph of chapter 1 to Dorothea, with
talk of her prospects and the possibility of her marrying. 'And how
should Dorothea not marry?—a girl so handsome and with such
prospects? Nothing could hinder it but her love of extremes, and her
insistence on regulating life according to notions which might cause
a wary man to hesitate before he made her an offer, . . .' Is Dorothea
being laughed at by the author? It would seem so: 'A young lady
of some birth and fortune, who knelt suddenly down on a brick
floor by the side of a sick labourer and prayed fervidly as if she
thought herself living in the time of the Apostles—who had strange
whims of fasting like a Papist, and of sitting up at night to read old
theological books!' A ridiculous girl, surely. Yet notice how this
paragraph concludes:

> Such a wife might awaken you some fine morning with a new
> scheme for the application of her income which would interfere
> with political economy and the keeping of saddle-horses: a man
> would naturally think twice before he risked himself in such
> fellowship. Women were expected to have weak opinions; but
> the great safeguard of society and of domestic life was, that
> opinions were not acted on. Sane people did what their neighbours
> did, so that if any lunatics were at large, one might know and
> avoid them.

The irony is here turned right round, away from Dorothea to the
society in which she lives and particularly to the male domination
of that society. The other side of *this* irony is admiration for Dorothea.

A moment later, the author is laughing at Dorothea again: 'Riding
was an indulgence which she allowed herself in spite of conscientious
qualms; she felt that she enjoyed it in a pagan sensuous way, and
always looked forward to renouncing it.' The mockery is, however,
indulgent, even affectionate. Finally, before we move into the

opening incident of the book, we are given an interim summing up of Dorothea's character in which, in spite of the humour, the implications of the irony at her expense are truly serious:

> Dorothea, with all her eagerness to know the truths of life, retained very childlike ideas about marriage. She felt sure that she would have accepted the judicious Hooker, if she had been born in time to save him from that wretched mistake he made in matrimony; or John Milton when his blindness had come on; or any of the other great men whose odd habits it would have been glorious piety to endure; but an amiable handsome baronet, who said 'Exactly' to her remarks even when she expressed uncertainty,—how could he affect her as a lover? The really delightful marriage must be that where your husband was a sort of father, and could teach you even Hebrew, if you wished it.

George Eliot is here telling us something of considerable importance about Dorothea, something which will explain her subsequent marriage and also her future relationship with Will Ladislaw. Though the tone is still humorous, there is a tartness at the centre. Dorothea 'retained very childlike ideas about marriage'. To put it in more modern terms, she was sexually unawakened and (this is made clear in more ways than one) did not even know what are often oddly called 'the facts of life'. Marriage for her was an ennobling discipleship to a father-figure. She had no idea of the kind of emotional or physical relationship that was really involved. It was to require a glamorous outsider to awaken her to some awareness of this, and critics who complain of the theatrical unreality of Will Ladislaw would do well to realise what is involved here. Will's place in the novel and the success or failure with which he is treated by George Eliot will be discussed later; but it is worth pointing out at this stage that the curly-headed Apollo-like figure of Will, confronting Dorothea in the sunshine of Italy at the very moment when she is beginning to realise the barrenness of her marriage to Casaubon, is an almost symbolic agent of release and awakening. That Will eventually captures Dorothea's love, as from this critical Italian encounter he has had her passionate interest, does not mean that we as readers are called upon to admire him or even that his creator admired him. Dorothea by her nature and her history had been conditioned to respond to that kind of person, and the moral implications of this are very ambiguous indeed. The important point, in reading chapter 1, is to realise that we are here being shown, with great delicacy but unmistakably, a nineteen-year-old girl who has completely sublimated her sexual instincts (of which of course she is wholly unaware) into an idealistic yearning for service. The first *fact* given us when the narrative gets into its stride is that the Reverend Edward Casaubon, who with Sir James Chettam is going to dine that day at the Brookes, has already aroused in Dorothea 'some venerating expectation.'

The chapter then moves into the incident of the two sisters and the jewels, in which the relation between Dorothea and Celia is suggested with the most delicate precision and an atmosphere of combined irony and indulgence plays continually about Dorothea. She treats Celia with an almost patronising affection ('What a wonderful little almanac you are, Celia! Is it six calendar or six lunar months?') but it does not take us long to discover that she is really the more vulnerable. And her concern for the preservation of her own superior morality is more egotistic than she realises. The devices which she employs only half consciously to keep her high moral tone with respect to Celia ('There—take away your property.' 'Nay, Celia, that is too much to ask, that I should wear trinkets to keep you in countenance') indicate a moral consciousness continually on the stretch. And the deep sensuous awareness which she possesses is fought down or transmuted to religious feeling with almost pathetic contrivance:

'How very beautiful these gems are!' said Dorothea, under a new current of feeling, as sudden as the gleam. 'It is strange how deeply colours seem to penetrate one, like scent. I suppose that is the reason why gems are used as spiritual emblems in the Revelation of St. John. They look like fragments of heaven. . . .'

The chapter ends, significantly, with the natural affection between the two sisters conquering their difference of attitude. It was Dorothea's impulsive assertion of moral superiority that had put her in the wrong, but she implicitly asks for forgiveness and is pardoned by the sister whose habitual attitude to her had always been 'a mixture of criticism and awe'. Which of these two sisters sees more clearly?

And what is the relation between clear-sightedness and virtue? These two questions are posed by this first episode, and they are to wind their way into the story in all sorts of ways.

When in the following chapter we meet Mr. Casaubon dining at the Grange we are given first Dorothea's way of seeing him. She sees him in terms of a portrait of Locke, and thus surrounds him at once with an aura of philosophical greatness. But when, alone with Celia in the drawing-room, she mentions his resemblance to Locke, Celia asks: 'Had Locke those two white moles with hairs on them?' This of course is another way of seeing. The girls exchange sharp words, Dorothea referring obliquely to Sir James Chettam, her admirer, as possessing 'the complexion of a *cochon de lait*'. She reproaches Celia for looking 'at human beings as if they were merely animals with a toilette', and never seeing 'the great soul in a man's face'. Celia replies with the critical question: 'Has Mr. Casaubon a great soul?' And Dorothea answers decisively in the affirmative— because 'everything I see in him corresponds to his pamphlet on Biblical Cosmology'. The remark is of course ridiculous in its naïveté. But it is truer than Dorothea knows. When, a little later on in the novel, we learn the truth about Mr. Casaubon's pamphlets, we appreciate that it is indeed true that everything about him corresponds to them—and that is his tragedy, and Dorothea's ordeal.

By this time Mr. Casaubon has told the truth about himself, again more profoundly and symbolically than he realises. 'I feed too much on the inward sources; I live too much with the dead,' he tells Mr. Brooke. We learn later that he has no true inward sources, so that in fact what it is saying is that he is spiritually starving as well as emotionally dead. The dead pedantic calm of his speech—a masterpiece of achieved tone on the author's part—reinforces this impression, particularly in its contrast with Mr. Brooke's cheerfully wandering garrulity. The contrast between Mr. Casaubon and Mr. Brooke enhances the characterisation of both. Mr. Casaubon 'delivered himself with precision, as if he had been called upon to make a public statement; and the balanced sing-song neatness of his speech, occasionally corresponded to by a movement of his head, was the more conspicuous from its contrast with good Mr. Brooke's scrappy slovenliness'. When, in chapter 51, we hear Mr. Brooke make his absurd (yet engagingly human) political speech, we realise to the full that here is a man who delivers a public statement as though it were private conversation—the precise reverse of Casaubon's habit. Brooke is 'good Mr. Brooke': if this phrase is patronising it is also well-disposed. Brooke is a figure of fun, and also in the contrast between his political theories and his economic practice, a man guilty of culpable folly; yet in a sense never specified but towards which the movement of the novel keeps directing us, he is on the side of life as Casaubon is not.

Dorothea's misinterpretations of Casaubon are linked by the author to that kind of large, unwarranted inference on which social institutions in some degree depend. In telling us how much Dorothea took out of a dry and formal remark of Casaubon's she adds: 'but really life could never have gone on in any period but for this liberal allowance of conclusions, which has facilitated marriage under the difficulties of civilisation'. This is only partly ironical. The remark contains a serious suggestion that we should not make unrealistic claims on life. The suggestion excuses Dorothea in this instance, yet (and here is another kind of irony) Dorothea is the character who is making unrealistic claims on life.

We are not allowed to forget the two radically conflicting views of Casaubon: Celia escapes from 'Mr. Casaubon's moles and sallowness' and Dorothea, seeing reflected in Mr. Casaubon's mind 'in vague labyrinthine extension every quality she herself brought', compares his manner of instruction to that of Milton's Raphael to Adam. It is in this third chapter that we first learn of Casaubon's life's work, an attempt to show 'that all the mythical systems or erratic mythical fragments in the world were corruptions of a tradition once revealed'. It is interesting that George Eliot does not bring the intellectual resources of her agnostic mind to bear in showing the absurdity of this projected 'Key to All Mythologies'. The absurdity and, even more, the barrenness of the enterprise emerges through its being shown as bound up with Casaubon's mind and character; it is not something *inherently* ridiculous. Indeed, there is a presumption of the nobility of any enterprise which has as its aim the getting down to fundamentals, the provision of a unifying clue to much disparate material. Lydgate's research project first mentioned in chapter 15, the search for the 'primitive tissue', is of the same order. The question with which Lydgate is involved is: 'have not these structures some common basis from which they have all started, as your sarsnet, gauze, net, satin and velvet from the raw cocoon?' There is no doubt that George Eliot approved of Lydgate's research project and that when he is caught up in the web that means the end of his career as a researcher this is a tragic, or at least a bitter and unhappy, outcome. The parallel between Casaubon's and Lydgate's research, therefore, can only dignify Casaubon's. There *is* a key to all mythologies, the implication is, but Casaubon has neither the character nor the intellect to be able to discover it. It is not theological credulity, but lack of intellectual and imaginative power, above all, certain defects of *character*, which render Casaubon's research abortive. At all points in the novel qualities of character chiefly determine the success of enterprises posed by the intellect. Casaubon's lack of knowledge of German, which Will Ladislaw tells Dorothea prevents him from seeing how old-fashioned and useless his work is (in chapter 21), is shown as implying a lack of modesty and of imagination, not simply a linguistic deficiency.

Dorothea continues to interpret Casaubon's pedantic remarks— and all his conversation is pedantic; 'he had not two styles of talking at his command'—in the light of her own naïve idealism.

> 'He thinks with me,' said Dorothea to herself, 'or rather, he thinks a whole world of which my thought is but a poor twopenny mirror. And his feelings too, his whole experience—what a lake compared with my little pool!'

The water imagery is significant; it always possesses for George Eliot a suggestion of the deepest springs of life. But of course the truth is the reverse of what Dorothea supposes. Bit by bit as the story of her married life unfolds the imagery is reversed and Dorothea learns to see Casaubon not as a broad lake but as a dry and empty tomb. 'She longed for work which would be directly beneficent like the sunshine and the rain, and now it appeared that she was to live more and more in a virtual tomb, where there was the apparatus of a ghastly labour producing what would never see the light' (chapter 48). Images of dryness succeed images of water: 'such capacity of thought and feeling as had ever been stimulated in him by the general life of mankind had long shrunk to a sort of dried preparation, a lifeless embalmment of knowledge' (chapter 19). Above all, images of liberation and exaltation give way to images of confinement and narrowness. 'Poor Mr. Casaubon himself was lost among small closets and winding stairs . . .' (chapter 19). This development is finely anticipated in chapter 3, where Dorothea, still in her youthful mood of passionate idealisation of Casaubon, encounters check 'on one—only one—of her favourite themes.' This was Dorothea's love of building model cottages for farm labourers. 'Mr. Casaubon apparently did not care about building cottages, and diverted the talk to the extremely narrow accommodation which was to be had in the dwellings of the ancient Egyptians, as if to check too high a standard.' That last phrase, 'as if to check too high a standard', is the author's humorously satiric comment, yet it also suggests the idealising misapprehension with which Dorothea received this rebuff.

It is interesting to note how the same ideas received by Dorothea in her venerating mood are later to be revealed, to her as well as to us, as evidence of Casaubon's lifelessness. 'He was all she had at first imagined him to be: almost everything he had said seemed like a specimen from a mine, or the inscription on the door of a museum . . .' At this point 'mine' and 'museum' suggest to Dorothea 'the treasures of past ages' and 'mental wealth'. Later, they suggest burial and fossilisation. We feel at this early stage in the novel that Dorothea is being almost wilfully perverse in insisting on idealising this pedantic elderly man with white moles and 'a smile like pale wintry sunshine,' a man considered by the pleasantly normal Sir James Chettam as 'a dried bookworm towards fifty' and later, when he learns that Dorothea is to marry him, as 'no better than a mummy'. And when we learn that she looks to Casaubon for escape from a life 'which seemed nothing but a labyrinth of petty courses, a walled-in maze of small paths that led no whither' (which is precisely the imagery used later to describe Casaubon's life and work) we may wonder for a moment whether the author is not loading the dice, whether anything more than a story of Dorothea's ultimate disillusion can be made of this. We cannot respect or admire Casaubon, and we can only pity Dorothea's blindness. It is the measure of George Eliot's mastery of her material and her control of the reader's responses that, if we ever do have this feeling, it is evanescent, and that eventually Dorothea, and with her the reader, is educated by experience into pity for and understanding of this lost and lonely egoist. Further, the worldliness of the characters who surround Dorothea help to make her idealism attractive by contrast. Though we do not share her view of Casaubon, and clearly are not meant to—the chorus of disapproval is too general and too convincing, and clinched by too many particulars—we get a sufficient number of glimpses of him through her eyes to make us feel warm-hearted towards this schoolgirlish idealist. Indeed, Casaubon from an early stage takes on a certain pathos in the face of Dorothea's passionate misunderstanding of him. Who could live up to such innocent and ignorant expectations? 'It would be my duty to study that I might help him the better in his great works. There would be nothing trivial about our lives. Everyday-things with us would mean the greatest things. It would be like marrying Pascal.' There is irony here, and comedy, and at the same time a controlled pathos which plays around *both* characters.

As for Casaubon's expectations of marriage, they are surprisingly like what we learn later of Lydgate's. We are told in chapter 7 that he had 'made up his mind that it was now time for him to adorn his life with the graces of female companionship, to irradiate the gloom which fatigue was apt to hang over the intervals of studious labour with the play of female fancy . . .' Compare this with this account of Lydgate's attitude in chapter 16: 'Certainly, if falling in love had been at all in question, it would have been quite safe with a creature like this Miss Vincy, who had just the kind of intelligence one would desire in a woman—polished, refined, docile, lending itself to finish in all the delicacies of life, and enshrined in a body which expressed this with a force of demonstration that excluded the need for other evidence.' Marriage is seen by both men as the provision of a graceful ornament to their lives, and the wife is regarded as to be classed, as Lydgate puts it to himself, 'with flowers and music'. *Docility* is a prime requisite in each case. The differences between the two men's attitudes are, of course, equally striking. Casaubon's tragedy is that his wife soon comes to understand him all too well, Lydgate's is that his wife has no interest in trying to understand him at all. Casaubon is destroyed because he is found out; Lydgate, because his false expectations of what a wife should be combines with his own innate tenderness to trap him in an impossible situation. Lydgate's is the subtler tragedy, for he is betrayed by his virtues as well as by his defects. There are many parallels between characters and pairs of characters in *Middlemarch*, but none is simple or mechanical: the interplay of similarity and difference is an important part of George Eliot's method. The psychological and moral problems which face men and women are strikingly similar, but the personal situation is always unique.

We have already mentioned Dorothea's sexual innocence and ignorance. This is paralleled by Casaubon's desiccation. 'He has got no good red blood in his body,' comments Sir James Chettam, who has earlier called him a mummy (and been himself, by contrast, called 'blooming' by the author). Sir James's face assumes a look of 'concentrated disgust' when talking of Casaubon. Mrs. Cadwallader supposes that his 'family quarterings are three cuttle-fish, and a commentator rampant'. Casaubon himself is surprised to find, on abandoning himself to his 'stream of feeling' about Dorothea, that it was 'an exceedingly shallow rill'. (Another interesting water image.) The suggestion of sexual impotence, to match Dorothea's sexual ignorance, is irresistible. It is all very delicately done, and no doubt the Victorian reader failed to see in the relationship between these two the matching of impotence and sublimation. But *we* can see it, and we can appreciate how much this illuminates Dorothea's relationship with Will Ladislaw, the awakening agent. In this connection it is worth noting that in chapter 9 we are told of Dorothea's painful incomprehension of 'severe classical nudities and smirking Renaissance-Correggiosities' which stared 'into the midst of her Puritanic conceptions'. 'She had never been taught how she could bring them into any sort of relevance with her life.' In the light of this, her later meeting with Will in Italy in a context of Italian painting has an obvious symbolic function. Celia, who is soon to marry the blooming Sir James, first begins to feel really superior to Dorothea after Dorothea's engagement to Casaubon. 'Celia had become less afraid of "saying things" to Dorothea since this engagement: cleverness seemed to her more pitiable than ever.' The placing of this remark, which comes with a certain finality at the end of chapter 9—the last chapter before the scope of the novel widens to introduce Lydgate and the Vincys—gives it special significance.

II

In chapter 10 we first see George Eliot's deliberate attempt to cross the Dorothea-Casaubon story with other stories and to widen the moral, psychological and social implications of the novel. We take a second brief look at Will Ladislaw, whom Dorothea and we have so far only briefly met in restricting circumstances, and we see not only that Will's view of Casaubon ('plodding application, rows of note-books, and small taper of learned theory') reinforces that of Celia and Sir James but also that the author engages in a certain amount of irony at Will's expense. We are told of his 'generous reliance on the intentions of the universe with regard to himself'. Though in some degree Will is an ideal figure, as befits one who is to play the part of liberating agent for Dorothea, it is important to notice how often the author's irony is turned on him. In chapter 21, when Will's view of Casaubon ('groping after his mouldy futilities') threatens to sweep the reader entirely on to Will's side, the author quietly interjects the remark that 'Will was given to hyperbole'. In chapter 22—and these are the chapters dealing with the crucial confrontation of Will and Dorothea in Italy—Will's eloquent definition of what it is to be a poet is quietly punctured by Dorothea who reminds him that he has left out the actual writing of poems—'I think they are wanted to complete the poet.' In chapter 37 the vehemence of Will's reaction to Dorothea's marriage to Casaubon is toned down by the author's remark that he was given to a 'passionate prodigality' of statement. And in chapter 46, Will's fatuous pleasure at having been compared to Burke in a silly rambling utterance by Mr. Brooke is tied to the normal human tendency to welcome 'even a chance bray of applause'; the language is very unflattering. Even later on, in chapter 47, when Will's love for Dorothea is now a main strand in the novel, the author manages to associate his symbolic brightness with his actual fluidity of character: 'Sometimes, when he took off his hat, shaking his head backward, and showing his delicate throat as he sang, he looked like an incarnation of the spring whose spirit filled the air—a bright creature, abundant in uncertain promises.' That adjective 'uncertain' represents a deliberately cool qualification by the author.

It is in chapter 10, too, that George Eliot deliberately raises the question of point of view. Whose view of Casaubon is the right one? 'If to Dorothea Mr. Casaubon had been the mere occasion which had set alight the fine inflammable material of her youthful illusions, does it follow that he was fairly represented in the minds of those less impassioned personages who have hitherto delivered their judgments concerning him? I protest against any absolute conclusion, any prejudice derived from Mrs. Cadwallader's contempt for a neighbouring clergyman's alleged greatness of soul, or Sir James Chettam's poor opinion of his rival's legs—from Mr. Brooke's failure to elicit a companion's ideas, or from Celia's criticism of a middle-aged scholar's personal appearance.' She goes on to talk of the impossibility of even the greatest man's escaping 'these unfavourable reflections of himself in various small mirrors'. The image is interesting, and one which the author uses many times. If 'even Milton, looking for his portrait in a spoon, must submit to have the facial angle of a bumpkin', the implication is twofold: great men may receive distorting impressions of themselves if they regard other people and objects as means of seeing only themselves, and on the other hand would a really great man be interested in seeking only his own reflection? Should we not want to look out at the world rather than use it as a prop to our ego? The mirror image is, in fact, an image of egotism. And *Middlemarch* is very much concerned with egotism. One of the chief supports for the view of the novel which sees it as a *Bildungsroman* with Dorothea as heroine —and this is indeed one strand woven into the novel, though only one—is that the great moment of purgation and release which comes to Dorothea after her night of acute suffering on the apparent revelation of Will's faithlessness shows her being at last wholly *outward* in her idealism, not using others' needs as a means of satisfying her own idealistic ambitions. It is one of the most moving passages in the novel: Dorothea looks not into a mirror but out through the window into the morning light and sees a landscape with figures, people at work in a given time and place yet linked to the general human need to labour and to endure:

She opened her curtains, and looked out towards the bit of road that lay in view, with fields beyond, outside the entrance gates. On the road there was a man with a bundle and a woman carrying her baby; in the field she could see figures moving—perhaps the shepherd with his dog. Far off in the bending sky was the pearly light; and she felt the largeness of the world and the manifold wakings of men to labour and endurance.

One is sometimes tempted to wish that Dorothea's part in the novel might have ended here. But of course this is a social novel as well as a novel about the moral education of individual characters, and George Eliot had a social as well as an individual pattern to complete. Dorothea's marriage to Will, the outsider, is linked to other ways in which new forces from the outside disturb and threaten the accepted prejudices of Middlemarch, and her partial re-acceptance by the society which had rejected her, which is the theme of the Finale, is paralleled by that society's reluctant acceptance of other novelties—the Reform Bill, for example, and the railway.

If mirrors reflect the egotism of the observer, what of a man's un-reflected self? 'Suppose we turn from outside estimates of a man, to wonder, with keener interest, what is the report of his own conscious-ness about his doings or capacity: with what hindrances he is carrying out his daily labours; what fading of hopes, or what deeper fixity of self-delusion the years are marking off within him; and with what spirit he wrestles against universal pressure, which will one day be too heavy for him, and bring his heart to its final pause.' This kind of discursive author's comment is perhaps disconcerting to those readers who have learned about fictional technique from James or Joyce, but it is a perfectly legitimate device and is one of the ways in which George Eliot keeps expanding the moral context of her work. One of the differences between the novel and the drama is that in the latter no interpretative comment by the author is possible, which is why great drama tends to be poetic, since all the resources of language need to be called into play in order to suggest, imply or symbolise what the author is precluded from saying in his own person (it is significant that modern prose drama, Shaw's, for example, employs enormous stage-directions which are in fact novelistic de-scriptions of characters and motives). In the novel the author has a much more flexible relation to his material. It is open to him, if he wishes, to sustain 'point of view' entirely by presenting the action through the consciousness of particular characters. But this method, though the more modern, is not necessarily the most artistically effective. The test of the successful presence of the author in a novel is simply the way it works. In her earlier novels George Eliot sometimes distresses the reader by overt moralising or coy commentary; in *Middlemarch*, with one or two minor exceptions, she is wholly successful in weaving author's comment in and out of the action with sufficient tact and relevance to achieve an even-textured whole. The tone of her comments keeps changing—they can be ironical, quizzical, compassionate or straightforwardly moral. The direct moral comment is the kind least acceptable to the modern reader. But it is often either a *link* comment, showing the reader how to connect different elements in the novel and also how to connect the novel with his own life and indeed with life in general, or an anticipatory comment pointing forward to what the novel itself is to reveal with all the conviction of fully realised art. 'Mr. Casaubon, too, was the centre of his own world; if he was liable to think that others were providentially made for him, and especially to consider them in the light of their fitness for the author of a "Key to all Mythologies", this trait is not quite alien to us, and, like the other mendicant hopes of mortals, claims some of our pity.' This comment anticipates the actual movement of the novel, and it is our reluctance to accept it at this stage—for the reader here refuses to give Casaubon his pity—that makes our later involvement in Dorothea's compassion for her husband the more arresting and significant.

Chapter 10 first introduces the reader to important new characters, including 'this new young surgeon, Mr. Lydgate', and does so in an atmosphere of social gossip that reminds us of the intersecting circles that constitute human society in any given region. We are also made acutely aware of the question of social status, so central an element in Victorian society and so important in the ambitions of Rosamond Vincy and the placing of Will Ladislaw as an outsider. 'The Miss Vincy who had the honour of being Mr. Chichely's ideal was of course not present; for Mr. Brooke, always objecting to going too far, would not have chosen that his nieces should meet the daughter of a Middlemarch manufacturer, unless it were on a public occasion.' Someone remarks that Lydgate is 'well connected'. Thus themes are set going which are to be developed later in ways important to the total pattern of the novel. Chapter 10 ends with Lydgate's first impression of Dorothea:

'She is a good creature—that fine girl—but a little too earnest,' he thought. 'It is troublesome to talk to such women. They are always wanting reasons, yet they are too ignorant to understand the merits of any question, and usually fall back on their moral sense to settle things after their own taste.'

At the time this seems to stand as a valid criticism of Dorothea, as in some degree it is meant to be. But much later in the novel, when Dorothea intervenes with healing effect in the affairs of both Lydgate and his wife Rosamond, falling back only on her 'moral sense to settle things', we remember Lydgate's first impression, and the effect is half ironical, half confirmatory.

Lydgate's character is built up for us in stages, 'for character too is a process and an unfolding'. He is first presented, in chapter 11, against a background of the 'old provincial society' into which he had entered by coming to Middlemarch. This is significant, for the struggle with a complacent and reactionary society is part (but only part) of Lydgate's story. The movement of his fortunes is connected with his ability to confront that society successfully, without giving up any of his ideals. His eventual failure, marked by his departure from Middlemarch, makes a sociological point as well as a psychological and a moral point. But the social background presented here is more than the arena for Lydgate's struggles. It is a microcosm of all society, and the stress on inter-relatedness makes a point about the human condition, not only about Middlemarch. 'But any one watching keenly the stealthy convergence of human lots, sees a slow preparation of effects from one life on another, which tells like a calculated irony on the indifference or the frozen stare with which we look at our unintroduced neighbour.' This is the point put more generally. Put more specifically, with reference to *this* society, it becomes this: 'Municipal town and rural parish gradually made fresh threads of connection—gradually, as the old stocking gave way to the savings-bank, and the worship of the solar guinea became extinct; while squires and baronets, and even lords who had once lived blamelessly afar from the civic mind, gathered the faultiness of closer acquaint-anceship. Settlers, too, came from distant counties, some with an alarming novelty of skill, others with an offensive advantage in cunning.' There is hardly a phrase here which is not to be implemented in the action of the novel.

When we first see Lydgate he is already attracted to Rosamond Vincy. This of course is a useful device for keeping him from any emotional involvement with Dorothea, but it is much more than this: the relationship between Lydgate and Rosamond is to provide one of the central elements in the total pattern of the novel. The words first associated with Rosamond by Lydgate are 'grace', 'lovely', 'accomplished', 'exquisite music'. She seemed to have 'the true melodic charm'. Soon afterwards, more objectively, we are told of Rosamond's 'nymph-like figure and pure blondness', a way of describing her which is to be reiterated with deliberate insistence until the blondness becomes associated in the reader's mind with the frightening cool egotism which, as we are to learn, is her chief quality. The phrase 'infantine fairness' comes in chapter 12, and is echoed in a variety of ways later. 'Infantine' is the word that first lays down the suggestion of a creature not immoral or even amoral but pre-moral, with the unselfconsciousness of an infant who has not yet learned that the universe exists for other people as well as for himself. By a simple transference, Rosamond's blondness comes to have this suggestion too; her fair hair (and her gesture of patting it), her long neck, her 'silvery neutral' voice, all become, as the novel proceeds, aspects of her character as well as of her physical qualities. By linking her moral defects with her physical characteristics George Eliot subtly emphasises Rosamond's innocence, her inability to be different. For one of the most remarkable things about this brilliantly drawn character is that, while her actions are evil, destroying a good man, they are in a sense innocent. Her moral feeling, like her blond hair, remains infantine.

How 'good' a man is Lydgate, whom Rosamond in the end destroys? He is curiously like the Aristotelian tragic hero, a good man with a fatal flaw. Able, ambitious, progressive, courageous, compassionate, he nevertheless has 'spots of commonness' revealed in his attitude to women (whom he regards as means of elegant recreation and at most also objects of continuing protective tenderness) and his refusal to carry his progressive ideas from medicine to society. The fullest account of his character comes in chapter 15, after the novel is well under way, and its placing here, when we are already in some degree involved in his fate, gives it special reverberation. It is here that we are told that his 'conceit was of the arrogant sort, never simpering, never impertinent, but massive in its claims and benevolently contemptuous', and his 'vulgarity of feeling' is explained as involving a view 'that there would be an incompatibility in his furniture not being of the best'. His intellectual distinction 'did not penetrate his feeling and judgment about furniture or women'. But his faults are flaws in a noble character, and the reader is drawn into a sympathy with Lydgate's ambitions and his later frustrations which gives a special power to the scenes which present them.

III

By the end of Book I we have been introduced to all the principal characters, and the chain of events which is to link them and is at the same time to test their ability to achieve self-knowledge and a true vocation has begun. Book II is entitled 'Old and Young', and though the primary reference is to Casaubon and Dorothea, there is also a reference to Mr. Featherstone, Fred Vincy's old and ill uncle from whom he and others have great expectations, as well as to other characters and relationships. We get now our first clear view of Mr. Bulstrode, the religious banker, and it is interesting that our attention is first drawn to the way he *speaks*. Tones of voice play an important part in suggesting the moral potential of characters in *Middlemarch*. Bulstrode's speech is fluent and his tone 'subdued'. Of Lydgate, we are told that one of his 'gifts was a voice habitually deep yet sonorous, yet capable of becoming very low and gentle at the right moment'—a characteristic which removes him from Rosamond's 'thin utterance' as well as from the 'thin and eager' chat of parroting moralists (who are distinguished from true novelists in an interesting digression at the opening of chapter 15), and associates him with Dorothea, whose voice is low and musical.

Fred Vincy, one of those weak but agreeable young men so common in Victorian fiction, is brought at an early stage into an indirect association with Bulstrode, who is the husband of Fred's father's sister, because Featherstone, whose second wife was a sister of Fred's mother (the family relationships are important in the novel) says that

Bulstrode has accused Fred of borrowing on expectations of inheriting from Featherstone and Fred is required to produce a formal denial of this accusation from Bulstrode. The complex of individual ambitions, exhibitions of power, family ties, selfishness, and (on Fred's part) a sort of indolent optimism continuously outraged by the demands of real life, is brilliantly presented, and brings the reader right inside an element of the novel that hitherto has been presented somewhat externally. Featherstone asserting his power, Bulstrode asserting *his* power, Fred's weak good nature (and it is important to realise that his good nature is real; his genuine fondness for his mother is contrasted with Rosamond's neutral attitude from the beginning), Mary Garth's cheerful service, Rosamond's cold but deceptive vanity —these combine to work out part of a moral pattern in this section of the novel. Mary Garth, who (rather than Dorothea) is closest to the moral centre of the novel and closest to the author herself, has in her voice 'a suppressed rippling under-current of laughter pleasant to hear'—again tone of voice helping to achieve characterisation. The relation between character and achievement, so central in the portrayal of Casaubon, Lydgate, Bulstrode—indeed, everybody—is summed up with a fine moral precision by Mary in talking to Fred. 'Not of the least use in the world to say he *could* be better. Might, could, would—they are contemptible auxiliaries.' They are also the stuff of the novel. Lydgate's is a tragedy of might-have-been: Fred's is the story of man forced into discovering a vocation by pressure of external circumstances. Bulstrode thinks later in the novel, when his past is catching up with him, that if he had to start again he would be a missionary. Casaubon's character and abilities are unequal to his ambition. Dorothea can find no 'objective correlative' for her idealism. There is a kind of fatalism running through the novel: up to a point, character is destiny. Lydgate had enormous potential as a medical researcher, but Rosamond, his fate, was not the result merely of chance: she was a part of his character revenging itself on him. Dorothea might have been Saint Theresa in another age—but doubt remains as to the social usefulness of sainthood; may it not represent precisely that kind of unconsciously selfish idealism from which Dorothea is finally liberated?

The interview between Bulstrode and Vincy in chapter 13 projects with great vividness some of the major contradictions of Bulstrode's character. He, too, has his egotism, and looks for his reflection in others' minds. He 'ended by seeing a very unsatisfactory reflection of himself in the coarse unflattering mirror which [Vincy's] mind presented to the subtler lights and shadows of his fellow men'. The core of Bulstrode's problem, as it is to be developed in the novel, arises from the confrontation of conscience and reputation, and his final downfall comes by his loss of reputation. As he equates his reputation with God's cause, which he sees as progressing or declining according to how people think of *him*, there is a kind of hypocrisy involved. But it is not the gross hypocrisy of, say, Mr. Pecksniff in Dickens' *Martin Chuzzlewit*. We may be inclined to think so at first, but as the action of the novel proceeds we begin to be more and more aware of the moral ambiguities of Bulstrode's character. He parallels other characters in a disturbing way—even Dorothea, who is also committed to enhancing the glory of God through her own actions. And just as we are led eventually, as Dorothea is, to feel pity rather than contempt for Casaubon, so we are led in the end, as his wife Harriet is, to feel pity rather than contempt for Bulstrode. This modulation of our feelings towards characters of dubious morality is brilliantly achieved. The tradition of the novel up to this time had been to present characters in terms of simple black and white (think of Dickens, for example); George Eliot's combination of critical irony and sympathy represents a new and remarkable achievement in English fiction.

George Eliot leads us through different phases of feeling towards her principal characters through the sensibilities of another principal character rather than through her own overt comment. Dorothea's discovery of pity for her husband leads to the reader's similar discovery; the great humanising moment for Bulstrode comes when his wife goes down to him after she has discovered his disgraceful past and his present shame; and the helpless inevitability of Rosamond's selfishness is shown to the reader as making her pathetic and vulnerable by Lydgate's continuous reversion to tenderness towards her at the end of their scenes of mutual hostility. It is true that the author's comment often enlarges on the implications of such scenes; but it is not comment in the void, being directly related to concrete experiences embodied and fully realised in the novel.

Fred Vincy tossed between Bulstrode, Featherstone and his father presents a moral comedy of beleaguered egotism which weaves lightly among the other elements of the novel at this stage. But the main lines which we follow once Book II has got fairly under way are those of Lydgate and of Dorothea. The coming together of Lydgate and Rosamund is deftly done. We have already been told the story of Lydgate's early, impulsive love of the French actress Laure, and this new relationship seems to be the ultimate contrast. (We learn later—a characteristic George Eliot touch—that Laure and Rosamond are curiously alike. Laure killed her husband because he wanted her to live in Paris while she preferred to live in her native province; Rosamond metaphorically kills her husband because of a similar difference of opinion as to how and where to live. Lydgate himself becomes aware of the similarity later, and is preserved from rushing into a generalisation about all women, based on this similarity, by the intervention of Dorothea.) Laure had gone in for 'large-eyed silence', but Lydgate had lost his taste for this: 'the divine cow no longer attracted him, and Rosamond was her very opposite'. Again we hear of her being 'immaculately blond', her 'infantine blondness', her 'self-possessed grace'. Rosamond 'was a sylph caught young and educated at Mrs. Lemon's'. She was superb cold egotism given *finish*, in fact. The chapter ends with 'Poor Lydgate! or shall I say, Poor Rosamond!' Each, in ignorance of the other's dreams, related his or her view of their relationship to a separate and private ambition, and the two ambitions were incompatible. Lydgate had been merely amusing himself. He was 'quite safe with a creature like this Miss Vincy, who had just the kind of intelligence one would desire in a woman—polished, refined, docile . . .' Some day he would marry a girl like that: his immediate interest was in his research. 'But Rosamond had registered every look and word, and estimated them as the opening incidents of a preconceived romance.' Lydgate's good birth gave rise to certain day-dreams on her part, for 'it was part of Rosamond's cleverness to discern very subtly the faintest aroma of rank'. She was oppressed by the bourgeois position of her own family and by her mother's vulgarity: marriage for her was to be an escape into a higher social world. She had no interest in Lydgate in himself, her concern was 'with his relation to her'. The whole problem of the difficulty of real human contact is touched on here, as it is elsewhere in the novel. At the end of Book I George Eliot had commented on 'the difficult task of knowing another soul', observing that it 'is not for young gentlemen whose consciousness is chiefly made up of their own wishes'. The young gentleman was Fred, and if his self-centredness precludes him from knowing another soul, how much more so must his sister's: we have already been vividly shown the different kind and degree of egotism possessed by Rosamond. And now, at the end of chapter 16, we are told outright that Rosamond 'would never do anything that was disagreeable to her'. In all sorts of ways, direct and indirect, the author is weaving into the narrative the suggestion that these two people do not really know each other, and are *using* each other for their own mutually incompatible purposes. They cannot therefore both succeed in their ambitions, and it is already clear enough that Rosamond will win.

How Rosamond wins—at least in gaining her immediate objective, marriage with Lydgate—comes as a surprise, with a characteristic Eliotesque moral twist. For it is Rosamond's helplessness (not her cold scheming) and Lydgate's tenderness and compassion (not his sexual vulnerability) that finally bring the two irrevocably together. When Lydgate learns that he and Rosamond are being gossiped about, he thinks it best to stay away for a while, never imagining that Rosamond now considers herself as good as engaged to him. When, partly fortuitously, they come together again, he is suddenly made aware of her frustration and vulnerability, and flaring compassion turns (or seems to him to turn) to love. The great scene in Book III where they become engaged catches the reader as well as Lydgate in the moral trap which the author has prepared. Would we have Lydgate behave differently? The answer is surely 'no'—the reader is with him all the way in this episode. At the same time we are aware that Lydgate is caught because of his own weakness, demonstrated earlier, and his own thoughtless vanity. The scene must be quoted at length:

Miss Vincy was alone, and blushed so deeply when Lydgate came in that he felt a corresponding embarrassment, and instead of any playfulness, he began at once to speak of his reason for calling, and to beg her, almost formally, to deliver the message to her father. Rosamond who at the first moment felt as if her happiness were returning, was keenly hurt by Lydgate's manner; her blush had departed, and she assented coldly, without adding an unnecessary word, some trivial chain-work which she had in her hands enabling her to avoid looking at Lydgate higher than his chin. In all failures, the beginning is certainly the half of the whole. After sitting two long moments while he moved his whip and could say nothing, Lydgate rose to go, and Rosamond, made nervous by her struggle between mortification and the wish not to betray it, dropped her chain as if startled, and rose too, mechanically. Lydgate instantaneously stooped to pick up the chain. When he rose he was very near to a lovely little face set on a fair long neck which he had been used to see turning about under the most perfect management of self-contended grace. But as he raised his eyes now he saw a certain helpless quivering which touched him quite newly, and made him look at Rosamond with a questioning flash. At this moment she was as natural as she had ever been when she was five years old: she felt that her tears had risen, and it was no use to try to do anything else than let them stay like water on a blue flower or let them fall over her cheeks, even as they would.

That moment of naturalness was the crystallising feather-touch: it shook flirtation into love. Remember that the ambitious man who was looking at those Forget-me-nots under the water was very warm-hearted and rash. He did not know where the chain went; an idea had thrilled through the recesses within him which had a miraculous effect in raising the power of passionate love lying buried there in no sealed sepulchre, but under the lightest, easily pierced mould. His words were quite abrupt and awkward; but the tone made them sound like an ardent, appealing avowal.

'What is the matter? you are distressed. Tell me—pray.'

Rosamond had never been spoken to in such tones before. I am not sure that she knew what the words were; but she looked at Lydgate and the tears fell over her cheeks. There could have been no more complete answer than that silence, and Lydgate, forgetting everything else, completely mastered by the outrush of tenderness at the sudden belief that this sweet young creature depended on him for her joy, actually put his arms round her, folding her gently and protectingly—he was used to being gentle with the weak and suffering—and kissed each of the two large tears. This was a strange way of arriving at an understanding, but it was a

C

short way. Rosamond was not angry, but she moved backward a little in timid happiness, and Lydgate could now sit near her and speak less incompletely. Rosamond had to make her little confession, and he poured out words of gratitude and tenderness with impulsive lavishment. In half an hour he left the house an engaged man, whose soul was not his own, but the woman's to whom he had bound himself.

'He did not know where the chain went': we learn later that it is to go to bind Lydgate hand and foot. Yet he does not, to himself, appear to succumb, but on the contrary to assert a healing power. He is the doctor 'used to being gentle with the weak and suffering'. Rosamond's is now a 'timid happiness'. The association of Lydgate's role as doctor with his role as lover is—in retrospect at least—ominous. For all the moving charm of the scene, we are aware that this is not a proper basis for marriage, especially to a girl like Rosamond. Her happiness is 'timid' not because *she* is timid but because she is not yet quite confident that she has won. She makes sure at once. 'In half an hour [Lydgate] left the house an engaged man, whose soul was not his own . . .' How casually, yet how deftly, does George Eliot manage to link the idea of engagement with that of bondage. This is an odd consequence of tenderness. The teasing suggestiveness spreads out: life can be like that.

But we have pursued the Lydgate–Rosamond story beyond Book II: as the novel unfolds the different themes become more subtly linked, so that following any one in a straight line means omitting much and bounding ahead. Let us return briefly to Fred Vincy in his relationship to Mr. Featherstone. When, in chapter 14, Fred gets his long-counted-on present of money from Featherstone, it turns out to be less than he had hoped. The author's amused irony here reaches more than Fred. 'What can the fitness of things mean, if not their fitness to a man's expectations? Failing this, absurdity and atheism gape behind him.' The comic exaggeration is not merely mocking at Fred: it also strikes Bulstrode, who, as we are soon to learn if we have not realised it yet, associates his personal expectations with the fitness of things and the providence of God. What is a joke with respect to Fred is in earnest with respect to Bulstrode. When later events conspire to reveal Bulstrode's shady past and thus to frustrate his expectations, it is precisely 'absurdity and atheism' that lurk in the background. Bulstrode's response is, on a very different plane, strikingly similar to Milton's in *Samson Agonistes*: if the righteous are frustrated, is not God mocked? Surely it is not in God's interests to allow someone on His side to be publicly exposed to shame? Samson confesses, as Bulstrode well might in his agony, that his fall has brought on God

> Dishonour, obloquie, and op't the mouths
> Of Idolists and Atheists.

Bulstrode realises at last, and the reader with him, that this sort of reasoning is the last refuge of egotism—a more penetrating climax, perhaps, than that achieved by Milton.

One draws attention to a particular moment at a comparatively early stage in the novel and immediately the linked patterns of the story present themselves to the mind and one is led away again to a quite different episode. This is the measure of the inter-relatedness of *Middlemarch*; it is odd that Henry James could not see this, but thought the novel, though he admired it, diffuse and old-fashioned. Its 'abundant and massive ingredients', he argued, do not come together in an integrated dramatic story. James is put off by George Eliot's apparent discursiveness, her refusal to limit her point of view, her abundance of characters and incidents. But the careful reader has only to take up one end of a thread and he will find it leads him in and out, through character after character, situation after situation, and not simply in terms of the fitting together of the plot but in terms of the way the ironies and the wisdom work, of anticipations and parallels and illuminating reflections from one element to another. Take one simple moral point suggested often enough by the imagery: do we use other people as mirrors in which to see ourselves, or do we use circumstances as windows through which to look—really to look— at others? We have already pointed out where Dorothea stands in relation to this question. It can be asked of every major character, as well as of many minor characters, in the novel; and in answering the question of each one we become involved with all the others. The modulations of egotism—Fred, Rosamond, Lydgate, Bulstrode, Featherstone, Rigg—are part of the very texture of the novel. The most unlike characters echo each other: the most surprising moral

parallels exist; the most unexpected characters turn out to be heroes.
Is it Dorothea who shows 'duteous merciful constancy' as a wife? No;
it is—of all people—Harriet Bulstrode, whose response to her husband's humiliation, late in the novel, is clearly paralleled in some way
with Dorothea's response to her awareness of Casaubon's failure as a
scholar and as a human character. Dorothea it is true, learns to pity
her husband, but in the end she totally rejects his demands on her. She
is anxious, when she discovers that he is ill, to do everything to help
him and make his life easier. But she has no moment like that of
Harriet, when, after long brooding in her own room in order to
assimilate the shock of her new knowledge of him, she changes into
humble garments and goes to her husband to give him her trust and
compassion. And indeed even as between Dorothea and Casaubon,
it is the dried-up egotistical husband, not the passionately idealistic
wife, who achieves the finest moment in their relationship:

> 'Dorothea!' he said, with a gentle surprise in his tone. 'Were you
> waiting for me?'
> 'Yes, I did not like to disturb you.'
> 'Come, my dear, come. You are young, and need not to extend
> your life by watching.'
> When the kind quiet melancholy of that speech fell on Doro-
> thea's ears, she felt something like the thankfulness that might well
> up in us if we had narrowly escaped hurting a lamed creature. She
> put her hand into her husband's, and they went along the broad
> corridor together.

It is their last moment of communion, and concludes with a scene
curiously reminiscent of *Paradise Lost*:

> They hand in hand with wandring steps and slow,
> Through *Eden* took thir solitarie way.

This is the best that can be done with such a relationship after the
Fall, as it were. Yet there is so much more in this scene than that.
The comparison of Casaubon to 'a lamed creature' does more than
establish the *kind* of pity that wells up in Dorothea (it is not pity for
an equal). It helps to release Casaubon from blame, just as Rosamond's
'infantine blondness' helps to remove her from the sphere of adult
moral responsibility. The hurt animal and the helpless child—who

would have thought that Casaubon and Rosamond would ever draw together in the novel? The imagery brings them together, but not mechanically or superficially. The problem of egotism is linked with the problem of free-will, and lurking continually beneath the surface of the story is the suggestion that compassion is possible because the guilty are not wholly free to be otherwise.

When Dorothea walks along the broad corridor with her hand in her husband's—an illustration yet at the same time an odious parody of a true wedded relationship—she is re-enacting, in a better way, a previous scene. Earlier that same day Casaubon had learned from Lydgate that he might die at any moment, and he had meditated alone in the yew-tree walk full of bitter self-concern: 'his passionate longings, poor man, clung low and mist-like in very shady places'. Dorothea comes towards him 'and might have represented a heaven-sent angel coming with a promise that the short hours remaining should yet be filled with that faithful love which clings the closer to a comprehended grief'. ('Might have represented?' Whose point of view is this? Is there not some faint irony here directed at Dorothea herself: is this not *her own* view of her beneficent presence—not quite consciously, perhaps, but somewhere in her subconscious?) The rebuff is terrible:

> Mr. Casaubon kept his hands behind him and allowed her pliant arm to cling with difficulty against his rigid arm.
> There was something horrible to Dorothea in the sensation which this unresponsive hardness inflicted on her. . . .

It is this scene that is re-enacted differently in the walk along the corridor. The resistance came from Casaubon on the former occasion and his was the initiative in the latter. It is Casaubon, rather than Dorothea, in whom George Eliot is most interested in both these scenes. The effect on Dorothea of the withdrawal is noted, after which there is a sudden author's generalisation followed by a return to Casaubon. It is a characteristic movement, and worth noting.

> . . . it is in these acts called trivialities that the seeds of joy are for ever wasted, until men and women look round with haggard faces at the devastation their own waste has made, and say, the earth bears no harvest of sweetness—calling their denial knowledge. You

may ask why, in the name of manliness, Mr. Casaubon should have
behaved in that way. Consider that his was a mind which shrank
from pity: have you ever watched in such a mind the effect of a
suspicion that what is pressing it as a grief may be really a source
of contentment, either actual or future, to the being who already
offends by pitying? Besides, he knew little of Dorothea's sen-
sations . . .

The direct intervention of the author to enlarge the significance of
an action may be disconcerting to some modern readers, but this kind
of placing of a moment of the novel on the larger map of human
morality and human feeling is perfectly appropriate and is reinforced
by the novel's total movement. George Eliot is not pressing on to an
incident a meaning greater than it can bear; she is rather assisting the
reader how to read properly by suggesting the wider context to
which the novel refers. We may object that such assistance is unnecessary, and it is certainly true that on occasion it is so. But often it plays
a part in sustaining the tone, in preventing any premature taking of
sides, in clarifying the sorts of interest with which the story is presented to the reader, and in general in establishing a mutual commit-
ment to moral and psychological exploration by both writer and
reader.

An obvious example of author's intervention in order to ensure
that the reader is not falling into an over-simplified black-and-white
moral pattern in reading is found at the opening of chapter 29:

One morning, some weeks after her arrival at Lowick, Dorothea
—but why always Dorothea? Was her point of view the only
possible one with regard to this marriage? I protest against all our
interest, all our effort at understanding being given to the young
skins that look blooming in spite of trouble; for these too will get
faded, and will know the older and more eating griefs which we
are helping to neglect. In spite of the blinking eyes and white moles
objectionable to Celia, and the want of muscular curve which was
morally painful to Sir James, Mr. Casaubon had an intense consciousness within him, and was spiritually a-hungered like the rest
of us.

This brings the reader up sharp, and is meant to. Not that the irony
is lifted from Casaubon; but it is applied for a moment to the reader

too, in order to prevent him from making over-simplified judgments. The assertion of the author's compassion for Casaubon ('for my part I am very sorry for him') is accompanied both by imagery reducing him further to a contemptible egoist (his soul 'went on fluttering in the swampy ground', his sensitivity was of the kind that 'quivers thread-like in small currents of self-preoccupation or at best of an egoistic scrupulosity', his lot was 'never to be liberated from a small hungry shivering self') and by imagery which reminds us of his human reality and his human suffering. The author insists on keeping us continually morally alert, and unless we are continually morally alert we cannot read the novel properly.

IV

After Dorothea's marriage to Casaubon, the movement of her mind from idealistic hope to resigned frustration is charted rapidly and with remarkable specificness. Our first view of her as a wife is on her honeymoon in Rome, sobbing in her room in the Via Sestina (chapter 20). Images of narrowness and emptiness crowd on to the page, but at this stage they seem to reflect Dorothea's own limitations. The experience of Rome, 'after the brief narrow experience of her girlhood' was too much for her. We are reminded that she 'had been brought up in English and Swiss Puritanism, fed on meagre Protestant histories and on art chiefly of the hand-screen sort'. We are also reminded that she was 'a girl whose ardent nature turned all her small allowance of knowledge into principles'. She was thus not equipped to respond to Rome: it corresponded to nothing in her experience or could not be turned into principles or assimilated to the principles she had already formed. 'The weight of unintelligible Rome might lie easily on bright nymphs to whom it formed a background for the brilliant picnic of Anglo-foreign society; but Dorothea had no such defence against deep impressions.' George Eliot goes on to give a magnificent analysis of the effect of Rome, with 'all this vast wreck of ambitious ideals, sensuous and spiritual, mixed confusedly with the signs of breathing forgetfulness and degradation', on someone of Dorothea's background and temperament. The conclusion of the paragraph—'and the red drapery which was being hung for Christmas spreading itself everywhere like a disease of the retina'—is startling in its physical force. The image also reminds us of Dorothea's short-sightedness, which is mentioned several times as a literal, physical fact but which we learn more and more to see as symbolic of another kind of short-sightedness, the direct product of her idealising hopefulness.

It is, then, the impact of Rome on inexperience that accounts for Dorothea's unhappiness. Having made this point with considerable brilliance, George Eliot pauses before the fact of Dorothea's marriage. Was this also a factor in her unhappiness? 'Some discouragement, some faintness of heart at the new real future which replaces the imaginary, is not unusual, and we do not expect people [that is, her readers] to be moved by what is not unusual. That element of tragedy which lies in the very fact of frequency, has not yet wrought itself into the coarse emotion of mankind; and perhaps our frames could hardly bear much of it.' George Eliot is here being ironical about marriage, ironical about her readers, ironical about human nature. We are not to expect any of the conventional novelistic ways of handling marriage, evidently. It is a curious and effective pause, leaving the reader deliberately in suspense, before the author gathers herself together and fairly assaults the reader with evidence of Casaubon's inadequacy and of Dorothea's marital disillusion. It is not, then, simply Rome after all.

Dorothea's view of Casaubon was changing. But, mocks the author, surely he was just as learned as before? Dorothea had not really known him before. 'The fact is unalterable, that a fellow-mortal with whose nature you are acquainted solely through the brief entrances and exits of a few imaginative weeks called courtship, may, when seen in the continuity of married companionship, be disclosed as something better or worse than what you have preconceived, but will certainly not appear altogether the same.' Then follow the assaulting phrases and images which positively overwhelm the reader with a vivid sense of Casaubon's deficiencies. 'Stifling depression', 'anterooms and winding passages which seemed to lead nowhither', 'forlorn weariness', 'mental shiver', 'blank absence of interest or sympathy', 'lost among closets and winding stairs', and a characteristic use of water imagery to suggest the disparity between Dorothea's expectations and the reality: 'Having once embarked on your marital voyage, it is impossible not to be aware that you make no way and that the sea is not within sight—that, in fact, you are exploring an enclosed basin.' This imagery is reinforced by our exposure to Casaubon's conversation, with its chill pomposity of diction:

'Yes,' said Mr. Casaubon, with that peculiar pitch of voice which makes the word half a negative. 'I have been led farther than I had foreseen, and various subjects for annotation have presented themselves which, though I have no direct need of them, I could not pretermit. The task, notwithstanding the assistance of my amanuensis, has been a somewhat laborious one, but your society has happily prevented me from that too continuous prosecution of thought beyond the hours of study which has been the snare of my solitary life.'

Words like 'pretermit' and 'amanuensis' fall cold and lifeless in the pedantic sing-song rhythms of the prose. Casaubon's frightened self is hidden far below this repulsive camouflage of words. It is his second speech of about the same length; an earlier one, separated in this chapter by the image of his being lost among small closets and winding stairs, came in answer to Dorothea's attempt to get through to his real self, to find out what he himself really thought about the frescoes at the Farnesina:

'They are, I believe, highly esteemed. Some of them represent the fable of Cupid and Psyche, which is probably the romantic invention of a literary period, and cannot, I think, be reckoned as a genuine mythical product. But if you like these wall-paintings we can easily drive thither; and you will then, I think, have seen the chief works of Raphael, any of which it were a pity to omit in a visit to Rome. He is the painter who has been held to combine the most complete grace of form with sublimity of expression. Such at least I have gathered to be the opinion of cognoscenti.'

The tiny scared self remains concealed. The irony is the greater when we realise that this pedantic shuffling out of any responsibility to understand comes from a man whose life-work is supposed to be the provision of a full and final understanding of all mythology. Dorothea is led by her as yet only half-conscious fears to press him about his work: when will he stop compiling his interminable notes and begin to write his book? Casaubon, hit hard on his most vulnerable spot, responds with cold cruelty, snubbing Dorothea completely. The cruelty, it is made clear, is the measure of his own desperate fear of being found out by his wife. Even at this stage we have a certain compassion for the man who, having married for comfort and support, finds that his once humbly adoring wife is about to discover his central inadequacy which he has hitherto tried to hide even from himself.

To bring Will in at this stage was a masterstroke: it is to oppose the sun-god to the ice-god. But we must not make the mistake, here or elsewhere, of taking Dorothea's view of Will as wholly identical with the author's. The introductory dialogue between Will and Naumann establishes Will as something of a playboy of the arts. His talk about art with Dorothea has not the same function of Klesmer's great confrontation of Gwendolen Harleth in *Daniel Deronda*, when he explains to her how hard the true service of art really is. Klesmer is trying to make Gwendolen see her own irresponsibility and shallowness, is trying to shock her into some moral maturity. Will, on the other hand, is trying to release some of Dorothea's repressed sensuous awareness; or rather, this is what he succeeds in doing, as well as in sowing further distrust of Casaubon, but his aim is largely egotistical, to make himself feel good in his relation with Dorothea. Dorothea is absolutely ripe for impression by a handsome and arty young man. This does not mean that the author's sympathy is withheld from Will. Clearly, he is a hero of a kind. Yet his later adventures in Middlemarch are often treated by George Eliot with an amused air; if criticism is waived (and sometimes it is not) that is, we feel, because of the author's indulgence. Sometimes we see him transfigured by Dorothea's feelings towards him; sometimes he is an almost purely symbolic figure of release and fulfilment; in the end he manages to combine, in a rather mechanical way, aesthetic sensitivity, human understanding, and zeal for the public good, which might well be George Eliot's formula for the ideal husband. He is never fully realised, but he serves his purpose in the novel. Dorothea's shortsightedness is only partly cured by experience, and the girl who married Casaubon to her friends' astonishment is not so very different from the girl who marries Will Ladislaw to her friends' disgust.

Some critics have written of Will as though he is being proposed by the author as in all circumstances the ideal husband of the ideal woman. This is grossly to over-simplify George Eliot's art. We are never left in doubt of the fact that Dorothea's actions are restricted by the time and place and circumstances in which she lives: that, indeed, is the theme of the Prelude. Will is what time and place and circumstances offer, ideal for Dorothea only in this context. Of course, one might object to George Eliot's rather facile use of his foreignness, implying that exotic outsiders are those with true sensibility, and the somewhat Dickensian melodrama which ties him up with Raffles and Bulstrode, and the objection is valid up to a point. The novel, however, is rich and strong enough to assimilate this, and the reader's discomfort is transient.

In considering Will's foreignness one must remember also the larger theme of the impact of outsiders and of outside forces on Middlemarch. Lydgate, too, is an outsider, and is defeated by Middlemarch in the end. So, in a very different way, is Bulstrode, and so are the men who come to survey the ground for the new railway (but they represent the future, like the Reform Bill, and are not defeated). The xenophobia and resistance to change exhibited by so many of the minor characters in the novel are an important part of its total statement. We remember the sub-title, 'A Study of Provincial Life'. The network of inter-relationships, habits and prejudices which make up provincial life oppose themselves, sometimes successfully and sometimes unsuccessfully, to a variety of forces that threaten from the outside. Will is later compared by Mrs. Cadwallader, the guardian of the old social order, to an Italian with white mice. This is tradition defending itself from innovation, the establishment hitting back at alien infiltration, and we note it with both amusement and understanding. The reader is meant to disagree, of course. Yet—and this is the sort of question that something in George Eliot's art keeps provoking in us—does not the comparison reflect just a little on the real Will? However unkind and unfair, is there not just a touch of the itinerant showman about Will? Dorothea, naturally, would not admit this for a moment; but may not the reader do so?

The confrontation of Will and Casaubon in Rome is emphasised by an overt use of the sun symbol which always lies fairly close to the surface where Will is present. When Casaubon comes home to find his wife and his young cousin engaged in conversation, he 'felt a surprise which was quite unmixed with pleasure'. Then we are told:

> The first impression on seeing Will was one of sunny brightness, which added to the uncertainty of his changing expression. Surely his very features changed their form; his jaw looked sometimes large and sometimes small; and the little ripple in his nose was a preparation for metamorphosis. When he turned his head quickly his hair seemed to shake out light, and some persons thought they saw decided genius in this coruscation. Mr. Casaubon, on the contrary, stood rayless.

Whose impression is being described here? Not Casaubon's certainly. Is it the author's? But consider the tone—the force of that 'surely', the humorous reference to classical mythology in the phrase, 'a preparation for metamorphosis'. Consider the dry sentence, 'Mr. Casaubon, on the contrary, stood rayless.' There is obvious ironic humour in the fact that whereas Casaubon has devoted his life to writing, in a particularly dead fashion, about mythology, his wife is here being assaulted by a real live myth, a sunny figure on the point of metamorphosis (and we think here, however briefly, of Ovid's *Metamorphoses*, that great repository of classical myth). The irony is far from being all at Casaubon's expense, however. 'Some persons thought they saw decided genius in this coruscation.' The language gives away a certain flippancy of tone, a certain refusal to commit the author to this view. Indeed, the view of Will which we are given here is not quite the author's and not quite Dorothea's; it is a sort of author's parody of Dorothea's view. Dorothea, rather than Will, is being gently laughed at. At the same time the Apollo aspect of Will is emphasised, and plays its part in weaving the texture of the story.

Chapter 21, in which the paragraph occurs, is one of the great chapters. By the time it ends we have seen the full movement of Dorothea's mind with respect to her husband almost to the point of compassion. 'As Dorothea's eyes were turned anxiously on her husband she was perhaps not insensible to the contrast, but it was only mingled with other causes in making her more conscious of that new alarm on his behalf which was the first stirring of a pitying tenderness fed by the realities of his lot and not by her own dreams.' With Will's help, she has found Casaubon out and, paradoxically, this leads her for the first time to consider him as he is, not as an object for the satisfaction of her own idealism. Meanwhile, as though to emphasise the difficulty of a really mutual human relationship, the emphasis falls even more heavily on Casaubon's egotism; such a phrase as 'a blight bred in the cloudy, damp despondency of uneasy egoism' suggests again the marsh imagery which is contrasted with the image of the wide ocean, implying at the same time pettiness, restriction and disease. Dorothea continues to wake up:

> Today she had begun to see that she had been under a wild illusion in expecting a response to her feeling from Mr. Casaubon, and she had felt the waking of a presentiment that there might be a sad consciousness in his life which made as great a need on his side as on her own.

The chapter concludes with a paragraph in which the author points the moral in a particularly suggestive manner:

> We are all of us born in moral stupidity, taking the world as an udder to feed our supreme selves: Dorothea had early begun to emerge from that stupidity, but yet it had been easier to her to imagine how she would devote herself to Mr. Casaubon, and become wise and strong in his strength and wisdom, than to conceive with that distinctness which is no longer reflection but feeling —an idea wrought back to the directness of sense, like the solidity of objects—that he had an equivalent centre of self, whence the lights and shadows must always fall with a certain difference.

This is related to that same mirror imagery which we observed earlier. Dorothea has learned no longer to seek from Casaubon a reflection of herself, a satisfaction of her own needs, but to see his objective self as it is, in all its otherness. D. H. Lawrence believed that in realising the mystical core of true otherness in one's partner one finally achieved perfect sexual love. For George Eliot such a realisation was linked not to love but to pity. It had never been love at all, for either Dorothea or Casaubon; each had idealised the other into a perfect server of his own needs, and was thus prevented from seeing the other properly. When they are finally forced to see each other as they really are, Dorothea's idealisation moves rapidly through contempt to pity, and Casaubon's moves at once to egotistical dread.

But, as we have seen, he has his moment of moral regeneration, isolated though it is. And Dorothea's feeling of compassionate helpfulness cannot survive her husband's continuous shrinking—shrinking from her pity, shrinking from her knowledge. Contempt, even hatred, lie always in wait. By the time of his death he had become nothing but a heavy duty, and after his death he became a dead hand clutching from the grave.

Book III is called 'Waiting for Death' and Book V 'The Dead Hand', and the reference in both cases is double. Featherstone's presumed heirs wait for his death with eager expectation and Dorothea waits for her husband's death with a dutiful determination to help him all she can. The dead hand of Book V first appears in Book IV, with reference to Featherstone, who chuckles 'over the vexations he could inflict by the rigid clutch of his dead hand'. The parallel with Casaubon's will, forbidding Dorothea to marry Will on pain of forfeiting all she inherited from him, is obvious enough, and pointed by the reference in chapter 50 to Casaubon's 'cold grasp on Dorothea's life', yet the implied parallel between Featherstone and Casaubon is unexpected, shocking the reader into a new sort of attention to what is really going on in the novel. Perhaps the most striking parallel—or contrast, rather—in the whole of *Middlemarch* is that between Dorothea's and Rosamond's reactions to the crises in which their husbands are involved. When Dorothea learns the true state of Casaubon's health, she bursts out in a passionate appeal to Dr. Lydgate: 'You know all about life and death. Advise me. Think what I can do. He has been labouring all his life and looking forward. He minds about nothing else. And I mind about nothing else——' We remember this when we come to the scene in chapter 58 where Lydgate tells Rosamond about his financial difficulties and with a rush of renewed affection pleads that they should 'think together' about what can be done. Rosamond withdraws completely:

> 'What can *I* do, Tertius?' said Rosamond, turning her eyes on him again. . . . Rosamond's thin utterance threw into the words 'What can *I* do!' as much neutrality as they could hold. They fell like a mortal chill on Lydgate's roused tenderness.

The contrast is with Dorothea and the parallel is with Casaubon, who also had been wont to respond to his wife's attempts to draw him into a mutually experienced affection by coldness and neutrality. And so the pattern weaves.

V

The Garth family provide an important moral centre in the novel and, though we may not fully realise it at the time, Lydgate is failing a moral test when in chapter 17 he dismisses Mary Garth when her name is introduced by Mr. Farebrother with 'I have hardly noticed her.' We are told specifically that he does not care 'to know more about the Garths'. Fred's love for Mary is an important point in his favour. Throughout the novel, attitude to the Garths provides a moral test; Fred is the only member of his family who passes it. Lydgate's failure here is bound up with a certain lack of imagination which in turn is linked with his kind of pride. 'He had always known in a general way that he was not rich, but he had never felt poor, and he had no power of imagining the part which the want of money plays in determining the actions of men.' Rosamond takes for granted that Lydgate will keep her in the style to which she aspires; she 'never thought of money except as something necessary which other people would always provide'. In this she is curiously like her husband, who takes for granted that he will continue to live elegantly until the pressure of tradesmen's bills forces him into an awareness of the important part played by money in maintaining the style of a gentleman. This is part of his 'commonness'—George Eliot is interestingly original in seeing a refusal to understand the economic realities that underlie class distinctions as a sort of vulgarity. This seems to reverse the usual view, but it does not so much reverse it as go behind and beyond it to trace the links between imagination, understanding and distinction of character. Dorothea is affectionately mocked by the author for her disappointment in finding that her husband's parishioners are comfortably housed and do not need her good works; this is another kind of sentimentalising of economic reality. Mr. Brooke, who preaches reform but allows his own tenants to go illhoused at inflated rents, provides yet another variety.

Attitudes to money are important in the novel. Fred feels that the world owes him a living (a milder version of his sister's fault) and lowers his character by joining the group of potential legatees awaiting Featherstone's death, and in her magnificently drawn picture of the grasping relations besieging the dying man George Eliot rubs in the importance of the *idea* of money, rather than the money itself, to so many people. Rosamond, by contrast, was not 'sordid or mercenary', nor was Lydgate. But to take money for granted is a kind of selfishness just as corroding to the character as to pursue it obsessively. Bulstrode has made his money by devious ways for the greater glory of God; Will refuses Bulstrode's money when the latter wishes to make financial amends to him; Dorothea thinks that her husband should give Will that part of his fortune deriving from Will's grandmother (who was Casaubon's aunt) having been disinherited; Lydgate is helped out of his financial difficulties by Bulstrode's lending him the sum he had offered to Will and Dorothea relieves Lydgate from the danger to his reputation resulting from this by letting him have the money to repay Bulstrode—money is clearly a potent force in the novel. Good characters often feel the need of it —Farebrother, for example, who lives on £400 a year until he gets the Lowick living. Fred's involving the relatively poor Garths in financial loss reveals some central aspects of his own and the Garths' character. Behind all this lies something like Marx's labour theory of value. Caleb Garth supplies the clue: we are told in chapter 23 that 'he could not manage finance' although 'he knew values well' and in chapter 56 that 'by "business" Caleb never meant money transactions but the skilful application of labour'. The moral implications of money are tested by its sources and its use: its proper source is good and happy labour (one thinks of Ruskin and William Morris here) and its proper use is social good.

George Eliot returns several times to Lydgate's taking for granted a life of elegance:

But it had never occurred to him that he should live in any other than what he would have called an ordinary way, with green glasses for hock, and excellent waiting at table. In warming himself at French social theories he had brought away no smell of scorching. We may handle even extreme opinions with impunity while our furniture, our dinner-giving, and preference for armorial bearings in our own case, link us indissolubly with the established order. And Lydgate's tendency was not towards extreme opinions: he would have liked no barefooted doctrines, being particular about his boots: he was no radical in relation to anything but medical reform and the prosecution of discovery. In the rest of practical life he walked by hereditary habit; half from that personal pride and unreflecting egoism which I have already called commonness, and half from that *naïveté* which belonged to preoccupation with favourite ideas.

Here we have the clearest of all the several statements linking social complacency with pride and with lack of imagination. And we have it in the context of Lydgate's forthcoming marriage to Rosamond who, a few pages further on, says calmly 'I never give up anything that I choose to do.' The coming together of Lydgate's complacency with Rosamond's calm selfishness is ominous. One by one the elements fall together. Lydgate speculates contentedly on his future wife 'who would create order in the home and accounts with still magic, yet keep her fingers ready to touch the lute and transform life into romance at any moment; who was instructed to the true womanly limit and not a hair's-breadth beyond—docile, therefore, and ready to carry out behests which came from beyond that limit'. In the same paragraph we are told that the following day he bought a more expensive dinner-service than he could really afford. But then 'Lydgate hated ugly things'. When Mrs. Vincy hopes it won't be broken, Lydgate replies: 'One must hire servants who will not break things.' And in the final sentence of the chapter we are told that Lydgate relied on Rosamond's 'innate submissiveness' corresponding to his own 'strength'. All this, in the light of what is to happen, is irony of almost Sophoclean proportions. At the same time it constitutes an explosive situation whose outcome can almost be predicted.

The progress of Lydgate's disillusion is charted meticulously. It is not until Book VI, 'The Widow and the Wife' (Dorothea and Rosamond), after we have been involved for some time with Dorothea's affairs and with Bulstrode's troubles, that we return to the Lydgates to find Rosamond criticising her husband for not paying sufficient attention to his cousin, third son of a baronet. He is in the process of realising that Rosamond is interested in his medical talent

D

only in so far as it gives him social prestige and that she would prefer him to be more like his stupid but well-bred cousin.

'The fact is, you would wish me to be a little more like him, Rosy,' said Lydgate, in a sort of resigned murmur, with a smile which was not exactly tender, and certainly not merry. Rosamond was silent and did not smile again; but the lovely curves of her face looked good-tempered enough without smiling.

Those words of Lydgate's were like a sad milestone marking how far he had travelled from his old dreamland, in which Rosamond Vincy appeared to be that perfect piece of womanhood who would reverence her husband's mind after the fashion of an accomplished mermaid, using her comb and looking-glass and singing her song for the relaxation of his adored wisdom alone. He had begun to distinguish between that imagined adoration and the attraction towards a man's talent because it gives him prestige, and is like an order in his button-hole or an Honourable before his name.

The story of the marriage drives on from this point with a frightening inevitability. In each conflict with his wife Lydgate learns to recognise more clearly 'the terrible tenacity of this mild creature'. 'What she liked to do was to her the right thing, and all her cleverness was directed to getting the means of doing it.' Between them there was 'that total missing of each other's mental tracks'. In 'the biting presence of a petty degrading care'—the piling up of debts—Lydgate found Rosamond uncomprehending and totally unwilling to give up anything. 'Lydgate was much worried, and conscious of new elements in his life as noxious to him as an inlet of mud to a creature that has been used to breathe and bathe and dart after its illuminated prey in the clearest of waters'—a most revealing image, combining George Eliot's characteristic water imagery with a suggestion of Lydgate as the frustrated *hunter* (whereas he regards himself as the frustrated lover). Rosamond's cold passivity is suggested both in characteristic incidents and in the language used of her. She falls back on 'quiet steady disobedience' to her husband. When he tells her that he has pledged their furniture as security and has no intention of accepting her suggestion that he should ask his titled relations to come to his financial rescue, 'Rosamond sat perfectly

still. The thought in her mind was that if she had known how Lydgate would behave, she would never have married him.' Her utterance gets even thinner than usual. But when the critical scene is
over, Lydgate, desperate in his need to exert tenderness if not to
receive it, turns to embrace his coolly accepting wife. Every such
scene ends in this way. The *modus vivendi* which they achieve is
most fully described in chapter 64:

> He went out of the house, but as his blood cooled he felt that
> the chief result of the discussion was a deposit of dread within him
> at the idea of opening with his wife in future subjects which might
> again urge him to violent speech. It was as if a fracture in delicate
> crystal had begun, and he was afraid of any movement that might
> make it fatal. His marriage would be a mere piece of bitter irony
> if they could not go on loving each other. He had long ago made
> up his mind to what he thought was her negative character—her
> want of sensibility, which showed itself in disregard both of his
> specific wishes and of his general aims. The first great disappoint-
> ment had been borne: the tender devotedness and docile adoration
> of the ideal wife must be renounced, and life must be taken up
> on a lower stage of expectation, as it is by men who have lost their
> limbs. But the real wife had not only her claims, she had still a
> hold on his heart, and it was his intense desire that the hold should
> remain strong. In marriage, the certainty, 'She will never love me
> much,' is easier to bear than the fear, 'I shall love her no more.'
> Hence, after that outburst, his inward effort was entirely to excuse
> her, and to blame the hard circumstances which were partly his
> fault. He tried that evening, by petting her, to heal the wound he
> had made in the morning, and it was not in Rosamond's nature to
> be repellent or sulky; indeed, she welcomed the signs that her
> husband loved her and was under control. But this was something
> quite distinct from loving *him*.

Even this way of life is threatened by Rosamond's writing for
help, against Lydgate's desire and without his knowledge, to his
uncle Sir Godwin, and when he receives Sir Godwin's letter of refusal, which gives away Rosamond's game, his rage surges over her.
But, as always, her absolute conviction that she is never to blame ends
by making him feel guilty, and the chapter ends with yet another

scene showing Lydgate reaching desperately for tenderness. The
cumulative effect of these scenes, each showing Lydgate a little more
beaten down, is tremendous.

> Lydgate drew his chair near to hers and pressed her delicate
> head against his cheek with his powerful tender hand. He only
> caressed her; he did not say anything; for what was there to say?
> He could not promise to shield her from the dreaded wretchedness,
> for he could see no sure means of doing so. When he left her to
> go out again, he told himself that it was ten times harder for her
> than for him: he had a life away from home, and constant appeals
> to his activity on behalf of others. He wished to excuse everything
> in her if he could—but it was inevitable that in that excusing mood
> he should think of her as if she were an animal of another and
> feebler species. Nevertheless she had mastered him.

The final scene between the two occurs after their story has been
complicated by Dorothea's intervention and Will's cruel forcing of
Rosamond, for the first time in her life, to feel the true impact of a
wholly other personality. Rosamond's flirtation with Will, fed by
wishful-thinking vanity on her part, had involved her, however
briefly, in other destinies, and the shock forced her back to her
husband. We are told in the Finale of the Lydgates leaving Middlemarch and of his becoming a fashionable doctor with rich patients
—a complete victory for Rosamond. But the real end of this story
of a marriage is in the subdued eloquence of the conclusion of chapter
81. Lydgate had asked Rosamond if Dorothea's intervention had
made her any less discontented with him:

> 'I think she has,' said Rosamond, looking up in his face. 'How
> heavy your eyes are, Tertius—and do push your hair back.' He
> lifted up his large white hands to obey her, and felt thankful for
> this little mark of interest in him. Poor Rosamond's vagrant fancy
> had come back terribly scourged—meek enough to nestle under
> the old despised shelter. And the shelter was still there: Lydgate
> had accepted his narrowed lot with sad resignation. He had chosen
> this fragile creature, and had taken the burthen of her life upon
> his arms. He must walk as he could, carrying that burthen piti-
> fully.

The achievement of making Rosamond at once intolerable and pitiable is remarkable. This coldly selfish woman, utterly lacking in all sympathetic imagination, devoted to her own way, genuinely convinced that she is always right, who destroys her husband in total lack of awareness of the nature of his abilities and ambitions, is by her very incapability of understanding others made worthy of compassion. She is incompletely human, and the lack seems to absolve her in some degree of responsibility.

There are two moments in the novel when Rosamond is forced to realise the full presence of another personality. One is the great scene with Will in chapter 78 when she, who 'had been little used to imagining other people's states of mind except as a material cut into shape by her own wishes', is made to feel with a searing directness the outraged frustration and anger of the man she had complacently assumed was really in love with her and with whom she was flirting for her own amusement. This brought her 'a bewildering novelty of pain; she felt a new terrified recoil under a lash never experienced before. What another nature felt in opposition to her own was being burnt and bitten into her consciousness.' The verbs 'burn' and 'bitten' are unsparing. And though we are morally with Will, we find ourselves almost in sympathy with the bewildered suffering with which Rosamond first encounters the reality of another's feelings. The second occasion when Rosamond makes such an encounter is altogether milder. It is in chapter 81, when Dorothea, still under the illusion that Will is in love with Rosamond and Rosamond with Will, visits her to advise and help her and so gives Rosamond the one opportunity of her life to act disinterestedly, when she tells the truth about Will and so restores Dorothea's faith in him. The gentle, emotional, outgoing approach of Dorothea's, even though presented by the author with the utmost sympathy and no trace of irony at all, is nevertheless overshadowed by the uncharacteristic act of restitution by Rosamond—yet another of those moral surprises which the novel has in store for us. Rosamond, of course, is in a sense still acting selfishly, making herself feel better in respect to Will, and she takes the first opportunity of letting him know that she has set things right for him. But this does not diminish her act. After all, in the very first chapter of the novel George Eliot had made clear some of the ambiguities of virtue and showed that the desire to feel good could not be dissociated, even in the most virtuous, from the motives which lead to good and unselfish actions.

VI

Fred Vincy's expectations from life are not dissimilar to those of the unmarried Lydgate which we have already discussed. But it was not pride or 'commonness' that produced them; it was his optimism, his easy confidence that with his bearing and education life was bound to do something to help him. 'That he should ever fall into a thoroughly unpleasant position—wear trousers shrunk with washing, eat cold mutton, have to walk for want of a horse, or to "duck under" in any sort of way—was an absurdity irreconcilable with those cheerful intuitions implanted in him by nature.' Fred is educated by circumstances into self-reliance—the circumstances being mainly the Garth family. Caleb Garth's position with respect to money and labour has already been noted. Caleb is used also to emphasise George Eliot's insistence that practical virtues rather than doctrinal orthodoxy are what really matter. This is a recurring theme in all her novels, and is important also in her portrait of Farebrother. Though Caleb 'never regarded himself as other than an orthodox Christian, and would argue on prevenient grace if the subject were proposed to him, I think his virtual divinities were good practical schemes, accurate work, and the faithful completion of undertakings: his prince of darkness was a slack workman'.

While there is certainly an element of idealisation in the portrait of Caleb Garth (George Eliot was thinking partly of her father) and occasionally a false note is sounded, as in the parenthetical 'pardon these details for once—you would have learned to love them if you had known Caleb Garth' in chapter 23, this element does not significantly diminish the effectiveness with which he and his family work into the pattern of the novel. Their accurate social placing helps to give them concreteness. 'Mrs. Vincy had never been at her ease with Mrs. Garth, and frequently spoke of her as a woman who had had to work for her bread—meaning that Mrs. Garth had been a teacher before her marriage; in which case an intimacy with

Lindley Murray [the standard school grammar] and Mangnall's Questions was something like a draper's discrimination of calico trade-marks, or a courier's acquaintance with foreign countries: no woman who was better off needed that sort of thing.' The slight tenseness in the relations between the Vincys and the Garths, so precisely realised in the scene between Mary and Rosamond in chapter 12, gives a moral as well as a psychological meaning to Fred's love for Mary, for it is an assertion of genuine affection in the face of class prejudice and of apparent self-interest. Yet Fred's moral position is for a long time very dubious, and it is precisely his juxtaposition with Mary and her family which reveals this. When his foolish optimism and bad judgment have lost him the money with which he was to repay the bulk of the money he had borrowed on Mr. Garth's guarantee, his immediate reaction is to consider himself unfortunate and ill-used. It was Mrs. Garth's brisk, uncomplaining, practical way of meeting the disastrous loss which this involved for the Garths which first makes him see the situation from another view than his own. (Again, we think of the parallel with Rosamond and the one occasion—of a very different kind—when she was forced to *feel* another's view. Fred is always shown as more educable in sympathy than his sister: the potentiality is there from the beginning.)

> But she had made Fred feel for the first time something like the tooth of remorse. Curiously enough, his pain in the affair beforehand had consisted almost entirely in the sense that he must seem dishonourable, and sink in the opinion of the Garths: he had not occupied himself with the inconvenience and possible injury that his breach might occasion them, for this exercise of the imagination on other people's needs is not common with hopeful young gentlemen.

The reproach to Fred is somewhat mitigated by his lack of imagination with respect to others' needs being ascribed to 'hopeful young gentlemen' in general. The implication is that this is a fault of his age and class, not deep-seated in his character. The change of his own view of himself in response to Mrs. Garth's reaction is immediate and drastic: 'he suddenly saw himself as a pitiful rascal who was robbing two women of their savings'. This is an important sign of grace. True, his egotism rises again soon afterwards, only to receive an even more severe blow from Mary.

'I wouldn't have hurt you so for the world, Mary,' he said at last. 'You can never forgive me.'

'What does it matter whether I forgive you?' said Mary, passionately. 'Would that make it any better for my mother to lose the money she has been earning by lessons for four years, that she might send Alfred to Mr. Hanmer's? Should you think all that pleasant enough if I forgave you?'

The repeated rising of Fred's egotism and its as repeated rebuff by Mary is half-comic, but the underlying seriousness—indeed, the absolute centrality—of the episode cannot be missed.

'I am so miserable, Mary—if you knew how miserable I am you would be sorry for me.'

'There are other things to be more sorry for than that. But selfish people always think their own discomfort of more importance than anything else in the world: I see enough of that every day.'

'It is hardly fair to call me selfish. If you knew what things other young men do, you would think me a good way off the worst.'

'I know that people who spend a great deal of money on themselves without knowing how they shall pay, must be selfish. They are always thinking of what they can get for themselves, and not of what other people may lose.'

Here, spelt out in the simplest and most direct language, is a moral problem with which every major character in the novel is, in one way or another, involved.

The Garth family are the most fully realised as a *family* of all the characters in *Middlemarch*, and it is this fullness of realisation that makes their moral centrality in the novel acceptable. Mrs. Garth testing her younger children in English grammar or Roman history as she attends to the cooking in the kitchen is one of those thoroughly established domestic scenes in which the Victorian novel excels. George Eliot could do this, as other Victorian novelists could, but with her it is not domestic comedy for its own sake, not merely an appeal to the reader's recognition or sympathy or moral approval or cosiness of feeling; it plays its part in establishing the moral pattern of the novel, and everything else that happens to all the other characters can, in one way or another, be related to the moral centre provided here. The point is worth repeating and emphasising, because so many critics, following the misleading Prelude, take Dorothea as the moral centre of the novel. The Garth family are the only major characters in *Middlemarch* (apart from the ineducable Rosamond) who are not educated by experience; they do not change. This is because they are already in possession of the moral education that matters by the time the novel opens. This is a significant clue. The Dorothea-Casaubon story and its aftermath, and the Lydgate-Rosamond story, are of course more important in the pattern of the novel's action than the Mary-Fred story or than anything which involves the Garth family, but the Garth family establishes the criteria to which most other actions are referred.

An important part of virtue, according to the view that emerges in the novel, consists in not making extravagant or vain claims upon life, yet at the same time in not lowering one's moral sights when one restricts any claim. This is most explicitly suggested in a remark about Mary:

> Mary was fond of her own thoughts, and could amuse herself well sitting in twilight with her hands in her lap; for, having early had strong reason to believe that things were not likely to be arranged for her peculiar satisfaction, she wasted no time in astonishment and annoyance at that fact. And she had already come to take life very much as a comedy in which she had a proud, nay a generous resolution not to act the mean or treacherous part. Mary might have become cynical if she had not had parents whom she honoured, and a well of affectionate gratitude within her, which was all the fuller because she had learned to make no unreasonable claims.

This is a very carefully balanced attitude and that the author's approval lies behind it there can be no doubt. In the light of it, what becomes of the Saint Theresa concept with which the novel opened? Surely it is now seen as a form of unreasonable claim on life, which it is the part of moral maturity to forego. Idealism is precious and

D*

valuable, but boundless idealism is a kind of folly, based on self-delusion. To set bounds to moral as to other expectations without becoming cynical is the part of wisdom, and it is the ties of personal relationships (love *and* honour) that enable us to achieve this balance. The whole novel can be read in the light of such insights, for the whole novel contributes to establishing them.

VII

Fred Vincy's egotism is of a straightforward kind, and susceptible to chastening; Bulstrode's is much subtler, and in the portrait of him that develops from the actions in which he is involved George Eliot provides her fullest treatment of this complex moral issue. She is concerned with the human drive for self-justification, and the tricks which it makes it possible for the conscience to play on itself. 'For the egoism which enters into our theories does not affect their sincerity; rather, the more our egoism is satisfied, the more robust is our belief.' We have already remarked that Bulstrode is no simple Dickensian hypocrite. With no other character does George Eliot take so much trouble to make the ambiguities absolutely clear. 'He was doctrinally convinced that there was a total absence of merit in himself; but that doctrinal conviction may be held without pain when the sense of demerit does not take a distinct shape in memory and revive the tingling of shame or the pang of remorse.' The confrontation of Bulstrode with the blackmailing Raffles forces the moral ambiguities of his own character on Bulstrode's attention precisely by enabling his sense of demerit to 'take a distinct shape in memory'. At the same time he looks forward and sees with horror the prospect of 'disgrace in the presence of his neighbours and of his own wife'. The profession of moral superiority has its own penalties: 'To men who only aim at escaping felony, nothing short of the prisoner's dock is disgrace. But Mr. Bulstrode had aimed at being an eminent Christian.'

The reader is allowed to follow with Bulstrode the retrospect that Raffles has forced upon him, and it is odd (yet wholly appropriate) how elegiac the passage in chapter 61 sounds as it goes back over

Bulstrode's early history. 'Again he felt himself thinking of the ministry as possibly his vocation, and inclined towards missionary labour. That was the happiest time of his life: that was the spot he would have chosen now to awake in and find the rest a dream.' We move on to learn of the gradual development of his method of padding his conscience with pleas spun 'into intricate thickness, like masses of spider-web, padding the moral sensibility; nay, as age made egoism more eager but less enjoying, his soul had become more saturated with the belief that he did everything for God's sake, being indifferent to it for his own. And yet—if he could be back in that far-off spot with his youthful poverty—why, then he would choose to be a missionary.' He had found himself locked in a 'train of causes'; at no point was any act of conspicuous evil perpetrated, but nevertheless evil was perpetrated by him. Now, after thirty years of respectability and of the assertion of moral superiority, the truth about his past was being forced on his own attention by being threatened with exposure to that of others. (Again, we have the suggestion of the mirror image: it is only when Bulstrode is about to see the reflection of his evil in the views of others that he begins to see its reality.)

Bulstrode's need for 'the spiritual kind of rescue' was nevertheless genuine, and if this meant hypocrisy, it was not the 'coarse' hypocrisy of popular fiction. 'He was simply a man whose desires had been stronger than his theoretic beliefs, and who had gradually explained the gratification of his desires into satisfactory agreement with those beliefs. If this be hypocrisy, it is a process which shows itself occasionally in us all . . .' Bulstrode, then, is not the Hypocrite; he is Everyman. This is what gives such power and centrality to the character as it emerges in the novel. Again and again George Eliot holds up the narrative to stress that his was no extraordinary case, and that the reasoning with which he padded his conscience is not peculiar to evangelicals. 'This implicit reasoning is essentially no more peculiar to evangelical belief than the use of wide phrases for narrow motives is peculiar to Englishmen. There is no general doctrine which is not capable of eating out our morality if unchecked by the deep-seated habit of direct fellow-feeling with individual fellow-men.' The sympathetic imagination is required as a guarantee of moral action whatever our doctrines. One can apply this principle to all the chief human relationships in the novel and one will find that it is stated in the action in a great variety of ways. It is implied also in the imagery: again we have the contrast between the mirror, which returns the self, and the window, through which one looks out to others. The further implication, that state of mind rather than doctrine is what produces true morality, also reinforces what is suggested elsewhere in the novel—by the character of Farebrother, for example. The point is made explicitly with reference to Bulstrode: 'For religion can only change when the emotions which fill it are changed; and the religion of personal fear remains nearly at the level of the savage.'

The dialogue between Will Ladislaw and Bulstrode at the end of chapter 61, when Will harshly rebuffs Bulstrode's attempt to make amends, begins by having the reader wholly on Will's side, but as it proceeds—and this is the kind of thing we have had occasion to note so often in the novel—the reader's sympathies shift insensibly at least some way towards Bulstrode. Will was being 'too arrogantly merciless towards a man of sixty, who was making efforts at retrieval when time had rendered them vain'. Will's response reflects not so much moral responsibility as his own egotism—he is not the author's, still less God's, moral spokesman here. But Caleb Garth, when he quietly but firmly refuses to continue to work for Bulstrode after learning about Bulstrode's past, does represent the operation of an impersonal justice. It is precisely this aspect of the scene that makes it sound artificial, as though enacted on a different level of probability from the rest of the novel. Caleb becomes larger than life and his voice sounds from outside the story:

'I am sorry. I don't judge you and say, he is wicked, and I am righteous. God forbid. I don't know everything. A man may do wrong, and his will may rise clear out of it, though he can't get his life clear. That's a bad punishment. If it is so with you,—well, I'm very sorry for you. But I have that feeling inside me, that I can't go on working with you. . . . Everything else is buried, so far as my will goes.'

The remark about a man doing wrong and his will rising clear out of it could not be made by anybody who did not know the whole Bulstrode story—could only be made by the author, in fact. All Caleb knows comes from the delirious remarks of the dying Raffles.

In the circumstances, George Eliot succeeds only in making Caleb sound like an insufferable prig. It is one of the few false notes in the novel.

The 'Two Temptations' of the title of Book VII are Bulstrode's and Lydgate's. Bulstrode's is the more terrible—the temptation to contribute to the rapid death of a very sick man because that man has the power to reveal Bulstrode's evil past. But it manifests itself so indirectly, and is succumbed to in a moment of such fogged consciousness, that the reader is kept if not in sympathy then at least in full and almost morbid awareness of Bulstrode's racked state of mind. Lydgate's temptation is more complicated; it is to accept a much needed loan from Bulstrode when, on reflection, he has some doubt of Bulstrode's motives in consenting to give it; and it is also to succumb to financial and other pressure and give up his research ambitions and medical ideals, which means giving up his integrity. Both men yield, and the way in which their fates at Middlemarch are intertwined is a masterly example of George Eliot's ability to give moral meaning to plot contrivance.

The complacent parroting of Bulstrode's guilt (and of Lydgate's supposed guilt) in Middlemarch gossip brings to the forefront of our attention the social and environmental aspect of their situation. So far we have watched Bulstrode's bitter struggles with himself, punctuated by an occasional interview with an accuser. Now we see, circling wider and wider, the effects of public knowledge, or half-knowledge, of his past; we see the image of Bulstrode that is given back by these shallow and in some degree distorting reflectors. But Bulstrode had always depended on receiving his reflected image, and he is therefore all the more vulnerable to its change. Lydgate, whose pride had made him less dependent on public opinion, is less vulnerable, yet only relatively so. Every man is in some degree dependent on his environment; the interconnections between the individual and society are multiple and fine-meshed; this is implicit in the very title of the novel and asserted and suggested in innumerable ways. Both men are forced out of the community which one had thought to dominate and the other to ignore.

The scene of Bulstrode's public denunciation is done with quiet cogency. Mr. Hawley's speech carries all the dignity of civic assurance—George Eliot is extremely skilful in capturing different tones of private and public utterance—and the pause which follows it takes us into the very centre of Bulstrode's traumatic response.

The quick vision that his life was after all a failure, that he was a dishonoured man, and must quail before the glance of those towards whom he had habitually assumed the attitude of a reprover —that God had disowned him before men and left him unscreened to the triumphant scorn of those who were glad to have their hatred justified—the sense of utter futility in that equivocation with his conscience in dealing with the life of his accomplice, an equivocation which now turned venomously upon him with the full-grown fang of a discovered lie:—all this rushed through him like the agony of terror which fails to kill, and leaves the ears still open to the returning wave of execration.

That this scene should end with Lydgate's being forced by his compassion and by the demands of the professional medical man in him to help Bulstrode out of the room provides not only an effective turn in the action—Lydgate is now firmly linked with the disgraced Bulstrode in public opinion as a fellow conspirator—but also another variation of the theme of the compassionate man's dilemmas and paradoxes which we have already seen developed in Lydgate's relations with Rosamond. And the end of the Bulstrode story, as we have noted, reverses expectation without doing any violence to character by showing Bulstrode and his wife achieving a relationship never achieved by Lydgate and Rosamond—or, for that matter, by Dorothea and Casaubon.

VIII

The final coming together of Dorothea and Will Ladislaw has sometimes been censured as a conventional romantic happy ending unworthy of such a great novel. This is understandable; a certain relaxation of artistic strenuousness, a lowering of the pitch of the work, seems to take place in the later stretches. But we must not be blind to the evidence of irony at both Will's and Dorothea's expense that persists right up to the end of the book, nor to the author's insistence in the Finale that marriage is not a conventional happy ending but 'a great beginning' (thus suggesting that no ideal resolution of Dorothea's problem has been achieved even in marrying Will). Will's decision to stay away from Middlemarch is treated at the opening of chapter 82 with considerable mockery:

When Will Ladislaw exiled himself from Middlemarch he had placed no stronger obstacle to his return than his own resolve, which was by no means an iron barrier, but simply a state of mind liable to melt into a minuet with other states of mind, and to find itself bowing, smiling, and giving place with polite facility.

And in spite of his vindication in the matter of his relations with Rosamond, he had behaved selfishly and recklessly: he had, in fact, though with different motives and in a different way, aroused in Rosamond expectations similar to those that Lydgate had first aroused in her. Lydgate's discovery of what he had unwittingly aroused in Rosamond produced tenderness which he mistook for love; Will's produced uneasiness. 'To a creature of Will's susceptible temperament—without any neutral region of indifference in his nature, ready to turn everything that befell him into the collisions of passionate drama—the revelation that Rosamond had made her happiness in any way dependent on him was a difficulty which his outburst of rage towards her had immeasurably increased for him.' This sense of Will's having got himself into a nasty mess does not—and surely is not meant to—increase our respect for his character.

We move from this scene to find Dorothea frustrated in her desire to do good:

What was there to be done in the village! O dear! nothing. Everybody was well and had flannel; nobody's pig had died; and it was Saturday morning, when there was a general scrubbing of floors and door-stones, and when it was useless to go into the school.

So she determines on some improving reading, and tries in vain to learn the geography of Asia Minor. The author is still affectionate towards Dorothea, but this scene reduces her, good-humouredly enough, from a Saint Theresa figure to a rather silly schoolgirl. The culminating interview with Will comes immediately after this, in the same chapter (83). Both characters are rapidly restored to dignity by the nature of the scene which is now enacted: it is beautifully symbolic and at the same time utterly persuasive psychologically.

> While he was speaking there came a vivid flash of lightning which lit each of them up for the other—and the light seemed to be the terror of a hopeless love. Dorothea darted instantaneously from the window; Will followed her, seizing her hand with a spasmodic movement; and so they stood, with their hands clasped, like two children, looking out on the storm . . .

They are two children in a stormy world. Both Will's impetuous romantic chat about art and politics and Dorothea's passionately idealistic desires to be of service are now admitted, and at the same time dignified, as qualities of children. Yet Dorothea has learned from experience; indeed, they both have. The child image is ambiguous. Rosamond, too, we remember, with her 'infantine blondness' constantly reiterated, is associated with childhood. Childhood is innocence, and it is also total self-centredness: Will's and Dorothea's are the first, Rosamond's the second. The innocence of this couple is not incompatible with their having learned from experience; it suggests rather a certain incompatibility with the ordinariness and the compromises of the workaday world. Yet even in this symbolic scene Will is not spared. There is after all a touch of Rosamond's kind of childishness about him. The egotism of his angry insistence to Dorothea that his life is maimed and his refusal to consider any possible hope or comfort (for himself; he is less concerned with her) is blatant. In the end, it is she who has to propose to him. The chapter ends with Dorothea insisting on how little she wants.

The child image had been used with respect to Dorothea in chapter 76, in that scene which has sometimes been taken as an over-idealised picture of her behaving with perfect goodness as Lydgate's guardian angel. Dorothea urges Lydgate to explain to her the background of the events which have led to his being unjustly accused of complicity with Bulstrode and is confident that she will be able to put everything right. Everybody 'would know that I could have no other motive than truth and justice. I would take any pains to clear you. I have very little to do. There is nothing better that I can do in the world.' George Eliot's comment is worth noting:

Dorothea's voice, as she made this childlike picture of what she would do, might have been almost taken as a proof that she could do it effectively. The searching tenderness of her woman's tones seemed made for a defence against ready accusers. Lydgate did not stay to think that she was Quixotic: he gave himself up, for the first time in his life, to the exquisite sense of leaning entirely on a generous sympathy, without any check of a proud reserve.

Dorothea presents a 'childlike picture' in 'woman's tones'. Lydgate does not stay to think her Quixotic. What attitude is being conveyed here? Surely a deliberately ambiguous one. Lydgate's reaction, understandable and laudable in the circumstances, is not unreservedly the author's. If we have any doubts on this point, they should be resolved on reading a passage a little further on in the same chapter. We are still in the same scene:

> The childlike grave-eyed earnestness with which Dorothea said all this was irresistible—blent into an adorable whole with her ready understanding of high experience. (Of lower experience such as plays a great part in the world, poor Mrs. Casaubon had a very blurred shortsighted knowledge, little helped by her imagination.)

The tone of the sentence in parenthesis is unmistakable. When Lydgate rides away thinking that 'this young creature has a heart large enough for the Virgin Mary', it is perfectly clear, in the light of how the scene has been developed by the author, that though this represents a genuine, spontaneous and wholly understandable reaction by Lydgate, it is not, so far as the author is concerned, unmixed with irony. This, clearly, is not George Eliot swelling out the organ notes to convince us of the perfect goodness of her heroine. The whole procedure is exceedingly cool and the touch of amusement on the author's part is scarcely deniable.

The chapter following that in which we are shown Will's egotistical anger forcing Dorothea to do the proposing is followed by one showing Celia, her baby, her mother-in-law the Dowager and Mrs. Cadwallader. 'It was just after the Lords had thrown out the Reform Bill'—a hint of the background of public events which is capable of the widest interpretation—and they are talking of peers and rank.

Mrs. Cadwallader held that it was a poor satisfaction to take

precedence when everybody about you knew that you had not a
drop of good blood in your veins; and Celia again, stopping to
look at Arthur, said, 'It would be very nice, though, if he were a
Viscount—and his lordship's little tooth coming through! He
might have been, if James had been an Earl.'

'My dear Celia,' said the Dowager, 'James's title is worth far
more than any new earldom. I never wished his father to be anything else than Sir James.'

'Oh, I only meant about Arthur's little tooth,' said Celia, comfortably.

This world of moderate selfishness, moderate expectations, limited
horizons, and realistic adjustment to things as they are, has its own
attractions, its own validity, and its own norms. They are not ethical
norms, which are found elsewhere in the novel, but nevertheless they
provide their own kind of criticism of unpractical idealism and his-
trionic behaviour. It is the same kind of criticism as that provided by
Mr. Brooke who, foolish man though he is, often lays his finger precisely on what is wrong with some conduct that goes beyond com-
fortable normal experience. In chapter 28 he says to Casaubon: 'I
overdid it at one time about topography, ruins, temples—I thought
I had a clue, but I saw it would carry me too far, and nothing might
have come of it. You may go any length in that sort of thing, and
nothing may come of it, you know.' And nothing did come of it
in Mr. Casaubon's case. Another surprisingly acute remark by Mr.
Brooke is found in chapter 49, when, resisting Sir James's suggestion
that he ought to send Will away, he argues: 'As to gossip, you know,
sending him away won't hinder gossip. People say what they like to
say, not what they have chapter and verse for'—a truth that is abun-
dantly confirmed in the course of the novel. Or again, in chapter 7, he
reproves both Dorothea and Casaubon: 'But it's a pity you should
not have little recreations of that sort, Casaubon: the bow always
strung—that kind of thing, you know—will not do.' In the same
chapter he replies to Dorothea's confession of having sobbed when
she heard the great organ at Freiberg with the thoroughly sensible
observation, 'That kind of thing is not healthy, my dear.' This does
not prevent George Eliot from making Brooke a figure of fun: his
idiom is richly comic, and its confusions have moral implications

derogatory to himself, as his encounter with his poverty-stricken tenant Dagley in chapter 39 makes clear.

A final assertion of the claims of the normal and conventional is made in the last scene which brings Dorothea and Celia together. Celia now firmly believes herself the wiser:

> All through their girlhood she had felt that she could act on her sister by a word judiciously placed—by opening a little window for the daylight of her own understanding to enter among the strange coloured lamps by which Dodo habitually saw. And Celia the matron naturally felt more able to advise her childless sister.

It is true that the phrase 'strange coloured lamps' represents Celia's point of view, but the phrase 'Celia the matron' establishes Celia as someone fully involved in the ordinary concerns and rhythms of life, and this gives authority to her way of seeing things. George Eliot never fully commits herself to Dorothea's side in the conflict between the two sisters.

The sense of the claims of ordinary life arises also from the abundant detail which fills the novel, forcing on the reader an awareness of the intersecting circles of activity which involve people with each other, individuals with the community, a given moment of time with history, and particular human ambitions and foibles with the human condition in general. George Eliot's acute ear for differences in conversational idiom—consider, for example, the splendid talk of Mr. Trumbull the auctioneer—gives her a means of emphasising human variety and at the same time of linking that variety with a central moral pattern. Everything and everybody is *placed* in the novel, not only in time and space but in its own individuality and its relation to other individualities. Social class is used to give both definition and relationship to individuals, and a man's business or profession or occupation reflects both on the man himself and on the community in which he lives. George Eliot gives us a fully realised awareness of people at work in a way that no previous English novelist had done. Previously the novel had been concerned with people away from the ordinary rhythms of life and work. Even Chaucer's pilgrims are only seen on holiday; the picaresque novelists of the eighteenth century galloped their characters about the countryside without letting us really see them at their daily work; Jane Austen's principal characters are ladies and gentlemen of leisure; Dickens' characters, when they are shown at work, are shown perched on ridiculous stools in grotesque offices engaged in fantastic employments or in some other way only symbolically working. But George Eliot knew what a doctor's life and studies were really like (she read the medical journals to find out); she understood the problems of the banker and the landlord; she was aware of the difficulties of the scholar who wanted to make a name for himself by originality as well as she knew the daily routine of the estate-manager and the auctioneer. And she brought all this knowledge into *Middlemarch* with a deep sense of what a society at work was really like, and what problems for human character were involved in the structure of society, its needs in terms of labour and skills, and its involvement in historical change. Further, she was the first English novelist to be in the vanguard of the thought of her day. Long before she became a novelist she had been involved in the avant-garde thought of her time. She brought all the resources of a well-stocked mind and a large part of the knowledge available to the best minds of her generation to the writing of fiction.

Above all, she was an *artist*, and never more supremely so than in *Middlemarch*. Something has been said here of her interweaving of the various themes of the novel and of her use of imagery in establishing her basic pattern of meaning. Much more could be said. For example, a careful analysis of the different ways in which Lowick is described at different points in the development of Dorothea's relationship first to Casaubon and then to Will Ladislaw will reveal how delicately George Eliot reinforces the suggestions of the action by her methods of describing background. The 'grey but dry November morning' of her first visit (chapter 90), with first a sunless stillness and then, when the sun comes out, the avenue of lime casting shadows, has its own area of suggestion, quite different from, but related to, that of chapter 28, describing the Casaubons' return to Lowick Manor after their honeymoon, where such words as 'shrank', 'shrunk', 'ghost', 'ghostly' first arrest the reader before they are contrasted with 'glowing', 'healthful', 'gem-like brightness' and both related to and contrasted with 'tenderness', 'innocence' and 'purity'. Words march in cunningly wrought patterns through this chapter, but though they achieve their effect at once they are only noticed in this way after a careful reading. 'Dreary oppression', 'withering', 'shrinking', 'deadened' pave the way for Brooke's airy but (as we have seen) significant 'and nothing may come of it, you know', and are contrasted with such phrases as 'blooming full-pulsed youth'. The chapter ends with Celia's regarding Casaubon's learning 'as a kind of damp which might in due time saturate a neighbouring body'. Investigation of the language of the novel, which can only be hinted at in a brief essay, shows the firm control that the author had over her material and the carefully wrought texture of the whole work.

In the end, *Middlemarch* resists formulation. Some attempt has been made here to suggest the moral ideas around which the action is constructed and the interweaving fates of the characters developed. But the novel is richer than any moral formula. There are contradictions in it, but they are contradictions and not confusions; they suggest the richness and many-sidedness of life and the different sorts of norms with reference to which life can be illuminatingly presented. 'Illumination' is perhaps the key word. *Middlemarch* illuminates experience as much today as it ever did.

Select Bibliography

BIOGRAPHY AND LETTERS

George Eliot's Life as Related in Her Letters and Journals, arranged and edited by J. W. Cross, 3 vols., Edinburgh and London, 1885.

The George Eliot Letters, edited by Gordon S. Haight, 7 vols., New Haven, Connecticut, 1954–5.

CRITICISM

Jerome Beaty, *'Middlemarch' from Notebook to Novel*, Urbana, Illinois, 1962.

Joan Bennett, *George Eliot: Her Mind and Art*, Cambridge, 1948.

Barbara Hardy, *The Novels of George Eliot*, London, 1959.

W. J. Harvey, *The Art of George Eliot*, London, 1961.

Henry James, *Middlemarch* (most conveniently found in *The House of Fiction*, ed. Leon Edel, London, 1957).

F. R. Leavis, *The Great Tradition*, London, 1948.

Index